A Vicennium of Trivia

by
Justin Bohardt

Courtesy of

The Ministry of Triva

A Vicennium of Trivia
Justin Bohardt
Kindle Edition
Copyright 2023 Justin Bohardt

Dedication

To Anyone Who Knew What a Vicennium Is…

And I don't include myself in that. I had to Google it.

*In case you are still wondering and would prefer I tell you
rather than Google,
then cheers to you!*

A Vicennium is the measurement term for 20 years, in this case 2001-2020.

Hear Ye! Hear Ye! Hear Ye!

This unit of inquisitorial entertainment,

arranged for your compulsory enjoyment,

is brought to you by:

The Ministry of Trivia

(pause for polite applause)

in concordance with

any local acts

or pertinent parliamentary procedures.

A Vicennium of Trivia

by

Justin Bohardt

𝔍𝔫 2001…

1) These two companies, representing the potentialities of new and old media to a certain extent, merge, bringing together two companies with a combined value of $360 billion, the largest merger of all time.

2) Five members of the Falun Gong movement commit suicide by this means in Tiananmen Square in Beijing.

3) Investor and entrepreneur Dennis Tito pays $20 million to becomes the first tourist to visit here, thereby inventing a new industry to cater to the extremely wealthy.

4) Nine members of the royal family of this country are killed by Crown Prince Dipendra, who then turns his weapon on himself. This official explanation is disputed as Dipendra shot himself in the left side of his head despite being right-handed, and there is generally little to no explanation for why he attacked his family.

5) This website founded by Jimmy Wales and Larry Sanger- and in no way used by this august publication from the Ministry of Trivia- goes online. Commonly considered a poor reference site at its inception and roundly mocked in both academia and pop culture, it is now seen as a resource that has democratized knowledge and made information more accessible.

6) This Israeli politician, Leader of the Opposition in the Knesset, and future prime minister, visits the Al-Aqsa Mosque compound on Temple Mount in Jerusalem. His visit will be met with protests and riots which the Israeli police will put down with rubber bullets and tear gas. The conflict will escalate to the Second Intifada.

7) In response to the 9/11 terror attacks, the United States invokes this aspect of the North Atlantic Treaty, requiring all NATO member states to come to the assistance of a member who has been attacked.

8) This software from Apple is released and helps change the nature of how music is purchased.

9) An insurgency begins in the former Yugoslav country of Macedonia (now North Macedonia). The trigger point for the uprising in what had been the most stable of the former Yugoslav

countries is the repression of this language and associated flags and symbols.

10) A report in October 2020 claims that Philippine President Joseph Estrada and his family have received millions of pesos from operating this illegal Filipino numbers game. The allegations of corruption will lead to the Second EDSA Revolution which will peacefully overthrow Estrada.

11) Several former Kadogos, better known in the West as these, conspire to assassinate President Laurent Kabila of the Democratic Republic of the Congo. The motivation for the attack may have been retribution as Kabila was responsible for the deaths of numerous Kadogos, including having 47 executed the day before his assassination.

12) After terrorist attacks on government buildings, including the Jammu and Kashmir Legislative Assembly, result in fifty deaths, this country blames Muslim terrorist cells operating with foreign state sponsorship and musters forces in response. After a tense year, negotiation ends the conflict and averts nuclear war.

13) This American restaurant chain places a forty foot by forty foot target in the Pacific Ocean and states they will offer free food to all Americans if the *Mir* space station hits it when it crash lands in the Pacific.

14) Robert Tools becomes the first recipient of this fully self-contained organ called AbioCor. He survives for 151 days with it before passing from complications due to abdominal bleeding and a stroke.

15) John Kufuor assumes the presidency after defeating John Evans Atta Mills in the first peaceful transition of power in this African country since achieving independence in 1957.

16) NASA's robotic probe *NEAR Shoemaker* becomes the first spacecraft to land on this type of celestial body,

17) An outbreak of this disease in the United Kingdom results in the killing of approximately 6 million sheep and cows in an effort to halt the spread. This outbreak occurs on the heels of the Mad Cow Disease panic in the 1990s.

18) Despite international pressure, the Taliban begins the process of destroying these massive statues, carved into the cliffsides of the Bamyan Valley in Afghanistan.

19) The law known as the Act of the Opening Up of Marriage goes into effect in the Netherlands, making the Dutch the first to allow this practice.

20) This Westward-leaning Ukrainian Prime Minister is dismissed from office. He will run for president in 2004, survive an assassination attempt, and lose amidst accusations of election fraud. His defeat will lead to the Orange Revolution and a Supreme Court ordered re-do of the election, which he will win.

21) After a building permit is granted to rebuild the Ferhat Pasha mosque in this country, Serbian nationalists attack the cornerstone-laying ceremony, injuring 30 and leaving a pig carcass on the Muslim holy site.

22) Russian forces consisting of these special forces perform a zachistka operation- a house-to-house clearing operation in an urban setting- in Chechnya, leading to the death of Arbi Barayev, a Chechnyan warlord and underworld figure.

23) Riots develop in Bradford, England between demonstrators of the Anti-Nazi League and members of this far-right, fascist British political party.

24) Simeon Saxe-Coburg-Gotha, who ruled this country as Tsar Simeon II from 1943-46 before being ousted at the age of 9, is elected Prime Minister of the same.

25) After finishing shooting a music video for her single "Rock the Boat," this singer is killed along with eight others when her charter plane crashes shortly after takeoff. Investigations will reveal that the plane was overloaded and the pilot falsified records regarding his qualifications on that class of aircraft.

26) The United States and Israel withdraw from the World Conference against Racism over allegations of this in some of the conference's proposals.

27) Five are killed and 17 injured by letters containing anthrax spores sent to prominent American politicians, including this Senate Majority Leader from South Dakota.

28) Shares in this Houston, Texas based company plunge from nearly $91 to mere pennies in the wake of a massive accounting scandal which will become almost synonymous with corporate fraud.

29) This wanted man escapes from the Battle of Tora Bora and will not be found until 2011.

30) These two film franchises, both based off popular novel series by British authors, release their first theatrical offerings, which finish the year first and second in gross box office. One series currently has eleven films and the other six and one television series.

Random Fact, Fun or Otherwise

It is difficult to discuss the events of 2001 without mentioning the 9/11 terrorist attacks. While definitely falling into the otherwise and not fun category of fact, not addressing the attacks seems impossible given their effect on the world around us.

After the attacks, conflicts began as part of the global war on terrorism in Afghanistan, Iraq, Pakistan, Syria, Somalia, Libya, Yemen, Nigeria, Mozambique, Mali, the Philippines, India, Egypt, Indonesia, Burkina Faso, Niger, Russia, Israel, China, and Algeria. Asymmetric warfare, drone warfare, and the interconnected ties between terrorism, the narcotics trade, and human trafficking are all hallmarks of the conflict.

It is estimated that between 4 and 5 million people have been killed as part of the Global War on Terror and 35 to 40 million displaced.

Answers on the Next Page...

Answers

1) AOL & Time Warner
2) Self-immolation
3) Space
4) Nepal
5) Wikipedia
6) Ariel Sharon
7) Article 5
8) iTunes
9) Albanian
10) Jueteng
11) Child soldiers
12) India
13) Taco Bell
14) Heart
15) Ghana
16) Asteroid
17) Foot-and-mouth disease (Hoof-and-mouth disease)
18) Buddhas of Bamiyan
19) Same-sex marriage
20) Viktor Yushchenko
21) Bosnia & Herzegovina
22) Spetsnaz
23) The National Front
24) Bulgaria
25) Aaliyah
26) Antisemitism
27) Tom Daschle
28) Enron
29) Osama Bin Laden
30) *Harry Potter* and *The Lord of the Rings*

𝕴𝖓 2002...

1) This outbreak is first identified in Foshan, China, kickstarting a two year long pandemic resulting in over 8,000 cases and nearly 1,000 deaths.

2) President George Bush first uses the phrase "axis of evil" in a State of the Union Address, including these three countries in the axis.

3) Layne Stanley, lead singer of Alice in Chains, and this supergroup featuring members of Pearl Jam, Screaming Trees, Alice in Chains, and The Walkabouts succumbs to a long struggle with heroin addiction at the age of 34.

4) This famously neutral and isolationist European country holds a referendum on joining the United Nations. The referendum passes.

5) While campaigning for the presidency of Colombia, Ingrid Betancourt is kidnapped by this far left militia group. She will be held for six years before being rescued.

6) The death of UNITA leader Jonas Savimbi in this country, the second largest Lusophone country in the world by size and population, helps usher in an end to a civil war that has been fought since 1975.

7) Chris Ofili's artwork *The Upper Room*, composed of 13 specifically lit paintings of rhesus macaques propped up by elephant dung, premieres at the Victoria Miro Gallery. It will cause some controversy 3 years later when this British museum purchases it, a museum Chris Ofili serves as a trustee.

8) This country, occupied first by Indonesia since 1975 and then by UN administrators for over 2 years, receives its independence.

9) Despite never hitting the number 1 spot in box office returns, this independent feature from Nia Vardalos with a modest $5 million budget, brings in over $360 million worldwide, one of the largest hauls ever for a romantic comedy.

10) In Salt Lake City, Australian Steven Bradbury becomes the first man from this geographic area on Earth to win a gold medal at the Winter Olympics.

11) This former American president wins the Nobel Peace Prize for his post-presidency work. Many historians regard his post-presidency period more favorably than his presidency itself.

12) Terrorists, believed to be al-Qaeda operators, bomb the Israeli-owned Paradise Hotel in this country and fire two missiles at a chartered plane, failing to bring it down.

13) In the largest governmental reorganization since the creation of the Department of Defense in 1947, George W. Bush signs this act into law, creating a new cabinet position in the process.

14) The staging of this competition in Abuja, Nigeria leads initially to protests from both feminists and conservative Muslims. The protests turn to riots and religious conflict when a Christian newspaper, *ThisDay*, publishes an opinion piece referencing the competition and theorizing what Muhammad's opinion would have been of it.

15) Approximately 50 Chechen terrorists and 130 hostages are killed when Russian special forces attempting a rescue pump a derivative of this opiate, which is 50 to 100 times more powerful than morphine, into the Dubrovka Theatre in Moscow.

16) The last baiji, a river-dwelling species of this aquatic animal, dies in captivity, leading scientists to believe the species is now extinct.

17) In the 2002 World Cup, the United States defeats Mexico in the round of 16 by a frequent scoreline in USA-Mexico matches. The scoreline has become this taunting chant aimed at Mexican players by American fans.

18) Members of a purple-clad militia in the Republic of the Congo, named for these Japanese assassins, begin to assault government forces in the Department of Pool in southern Congo.

19) In celebration of Queen Elizabeth II's Golden Jubilee, this mayor of New York City asks that the Empire State Building be illuminated in gold and royal purple. The mayor states this gesture is a thank you for Elizabeth II ordering the *Star Spangled Banner* to be played during the Changing of the Guard at Buckingham Palace on September 13, 2001.

20) *The Spotlight* investigative journalist team at this newspaper publishes its first of many articles about sexual abuse in the Catholic Church and the cover-up thereof.

21) This treaty which allows for unarmed surveillance flights to occur in member nations' airspace, gathering information to be shared with all members, goes into effect. Treaty members are all European countries, save for the United States and Canada. Both the U.S. and Russia will later pull out of the treaty.

22) This video game, a collaboration between Squaresoft and Disney, is released for Sony PlayStation 2. Immediately, it becomes a critical and commercial hit and will spawn numerous sequels. By 2022, it will sell over 35 million copies.

23) The Organization of African Unity is re-formed as this successor organization.

24) As a part of this research project, Kevin Warwick surgically implants a microelectrode array in his left arm, allowing him to manipulate a robot arm via his own mind and the Internet.

25) The trial of this former president of Yugoslavia begins in the Hague on charges of war crimes and genocide. The trial will last until 2006, at which point the accused will die in prison.

26) This rapper's fourth album is released to critical acclaim and financial success, featuring singles, "Cleaning Out My Closet" and "Without Me."

27) Brazil elects this unionist metalworker and member of the left-wing Workers' Party to the presidency. After his first term of office ends, he will be charged with offenses related to corruption scandals in his administration and spend nearly two years in prison. In 2022, he will be re-elected to the presidency.

28) Fifteen female students are killed by a fire in this country. The deaths occur because the Islamic religious police will not allow them to leave the burning building due to their immodest dress.

29) A thirty-nine day siege begins at the Church of the Nativity in this city as members of the Israel Defense Force surround the church, trapping inside the 200 Palestinian militants who sought refuge there.

30) Oakland Raiders cornerback Charles Woodson sacks New England Patriots quarterback Tom Brady in a snowy playoff game, apparently forcing a fumble and sealing a three-point victory for Oakland. Referee Walt Coleman, however, cites this obscure rule and announces that as Brady's hand was moving forward as he was hit, the pass is incomplete and the Patriots retain possession. The Patriots will tie the game on that drive, and then win in overtime.

Random Fact, Fun or Otherwise

Steven Bradbury's "triumph" in Salt Lake City in the 1000m comes with a slight asterisk due to the manner in which he won. Firstly, one might argue he lucked his way into the semifinals as he failed to qualify out of the quarterfinals, but a fellow skater in his heat was disqualified after the race. In the semifinals, he was in last place against superior competition, but the three other competitors in the race all fell, allowing Bradbury to pass them and advance to the final. Bradbury was definitively the slowest racer on the track in the final, but a four skater pileup well ahead of Bradbury in the final turn allowed him to skate to the gold. It was a quite fortuitous series of events.

Which is not to say that Bradbury was not deserving of a few lucky bounces. He had won a bronze medal as part of the team short track speed skating event in 1994 at Lillehammer, the first winter Olympic medals for any Australians or anyone from the Southern Hemisphere. In the 1994 World Championships, he underwent a horrific injury where another skater's blade sliced through all four of his quadriceps muscles. He lost four liters of blood, needed 111 stitches, and came close to dying on the track. After a disappointing performance in Nagano in 1998, Bradbury broke his neck while training in 2000. Although his doctors told him he would never skate again, Bradbury was determined to skate in the Olympics a final time.

Bradbury has become something of a folk hero in Australia, and his name has entered the lexicon of Australian English. To do a Bradbury is to have some unexpected or unusual success. It entered the Australian National Dictionary in 2016.

Answers on the Next Page...

     Justin Bohardt

𝔄𝔫𝔰𝔴𝔢𝔯𝔰

1) SARS
2) Iran, Iraq, & North Korea
3) Mad Season
4) Switzerland
5) Revolutionary Armed Forces of Colombia (FARC)
6) Angola
7) Tate Gallery
8) East Timor
9) Southern Hemisphere
10) *My Big Fat Greek Wedding*
11) Jimmy Carter
12) Kenya
13) Homeland Security Act
14) Miss World
15) Fentanyl
16) Dolphin
17) Dos a cero (Two to zero)
18) Ninjas
19) Michael Bloomberg
20) *Boston Globe*
21) Open Skies Treaty
22) *Kingdom Hearts*
23) African Union
24) Project Cyborg
25) Slobodan Milosevic
26) Eminem
27) Luiz Inacio Lula da Silva
28) Saudi Arabia
29) Bethlehem
30) Tuck Rule

𝔍𝔫 2003...

1) Professional weightlifter and wrestler Kadhem Sharif Al-Jabbouri becomes famous for taking a sledgehammer to the statue of this man. His efforts will receive an assist from United States Marines and an M-88 armored recovery vehicle a few hours later, who bring the statue down.

2) Ilan Roman, the first astronaut from this country, is killed when the space shuttle *Columbia* breaks up on entering the atmosphere.

3) Tom Anderson, who is known ubiquitously as this, begins creating the first pages of a new social media site, one which would surpass Friendster in terms of popularity, but would eventually be dwarfed by Facebook.

4) Approximately 70,000 people are killed in Europe's worst occurrence of this climatological phenomenon since 1540.

5) A seventeen year long civil war begins in Sudan, commonly known as the War in Darfur or as this colloquialism, named after the model of vehicles used by both sides.

6) A new constitution is approved via referendum in Rwanda. Per the new constitution, at least 24 seats in the lower house of the bicameral parliament must be reserved for these. Eight seats in the upper house must be reserved as well.

7) Originally created as a prison for political dissidents, this prison outside Baghdad becomes notorious for the abuses perpetuated on Iraqi prisoners by American servicemen and women.

8) A computer bug leads to overloading issues at FirstEnergy, resulting in the second largest power outage of all time, spreading from New Jersey in the southeast of the affected area to this Canadian province in the northwest.

9) The first six-party talks are held between nations in an effort to curb this country's nuclear development program.

10) Akkala Sami, a language found in the Kola Peninsula of this country, is believed to go extinct as the last speaker, Maria Sergina, dies. In a 2020 census, one person will claim to still speak it.

11) After her husband Joseph Wilson writes an article critical of the Bush administration and suggesting that Iraq had not been attempting to procure weapons grade uranium, Valerie Plume's

name is leaked to reporter Robert Novak who identifies her as a CIA operative. Novak claims that he did not realize she was this kind of clandestine operative and that he was "outing" her.

12) American scientist Paul Lauterbur and British scientist Sir Peter Mansfield win the Nobel Prize in Medicine for their independent work contributing to the development of this medical diagnostic device.

13) A brutal shoulder-to-knee tackle from Will Allen tears all three ligaments in the knee of this University of Miami running back in the college football national championship game played in the Fiesta Bowl.

14) Martin Eberhard and Marc Tarpenning found this automotive company, even though it is more closely associated with their largest investor, who will become CEO in 2008.

15) American President George Bush stands on the deck of the *USS Abraham Lincoln* underneath a banner with this two word phrase printed on it as he declares victory in the war with Iraq. Insurgency and sectarian conflict will continue with American troops not withdrawing for eight more years.

16) This Presbyterian minister and children's television host dies from stomach cancer. In 2018, a documentary about his life entitled *Won't You Be My Neighbor?* will be released, followed by a Tom Hanks led biopic entitled *A Beautiful Day in the Neighborhood.*

17) The second and third films in this cyberpunk film series which began in 1999 are released. While not as well received as the original, the second film breaks *Terminator 2's* record for highest-grossing Rated R film. It will hold the record until the release of *Deadpool.*

18) A bloodless coup occurs in this former colony of Portugal as General Verissimo Correia Seabra arrests President Kumba Iala.

19) This Smashing Pumpkins frontman announces that his follow-up band, Zwan, has broken up.

20) Australian and New Zealand forces deploy to the Solomon Islands to help maintain peace in the face of rising ethnic and nationalist violence under the operational name Operation

Helpem Fren. Helpem Fren translates to "Help a friend" in this Solomon Islands language.

21) Under this operational name, inspired by a 1984 film starring Patrick Swayze and Charlie Sheen, American forces launch an operation that will capture Saddam Hussein.

22) This record producer and innovator of the Wall of Sound is arrested for the murder of B movie actress Lana Clarkson. He will be convicted in 2009.

23) At the height of this American television program's popularity, Ruben Studdard wins the second season over Clay Aiken.

24) The last flight of these supersonic jets occurs from London's Heathrow Airport to Filton Aerodrome.

25) This popular and long running role playing game series releases a direct sequel to a previous game for the first time, giving it the moniker "X-2."

26) This immigrant begins his third career (after athletics and entertainment) when he is elected governor of California (despite having trouble pronouncing California).

27) Chicago Cubs fan Steve Bartman attempts to catch a foul ball while Cubs player Moises Alou tries to make a play on it in the 8th inning of game 6 of the National League Championship Series. Alou is unable to make the catch because of Bartman's interference, and the Cubs proceed to implode, losing a 3-0 lead in game 6 and then losing game 7 to continue this curse.

28) Over $100 million in gold, diamonds, silver, and jewelry are stolen from safety deposit boxes in this European city, the hub of the world's diamond trade.

29) Earth loses contact with *Pioneer 10* when the craft's radio transmitter fails twelve billion kilometers from Earth or 80 of these measurements of stellar distance.

30) This American Secretary of State presents the case for going to war with Iraq to the United Nations. It will later be determined that elements of the Bush administration misled him.

𝕽𝖆𝖓𝖉𝖔𝖒 𝕱𝖆𝖈𝖙, 𝕱𝖚𝖓 𝖔𝖗 𝕺𝖙𝖍𝖊𝖗𝖜𝖎𝖘𝖊

The Curse of the Billy Goat is one of the more enigmatic curses in sports history. The curse began in 1945 when the Cubs were in the World Series, having not won the championship since 1908. During Game 4 of the series, the owner of the local Billy Goat Tavern, William Sianis, was taking in the game in the stands along with his pet goat, Murphy. Per the legend, other viewers we're becoming annoyed at the antics of the goat, and security asked Sianis (and Murphy) to leave. Supposedly, Sianis's response was, "Them Cubs, they ain't gonna win no more."

The Cubs lost the 1945 World Series, 4 games to 3, and between 1945 and 2015, they did not even make the World Series, let alone win it. They did not even make the playoffs again until 1984. The Cubs failed to advance in the playoffs in 1984, 1989, and 1998, which brings us to 2003 and Steve Bartman.

In the first round of the playoffs, the Cubs defeated the Atlanta Braves, advancing in a playoff series for the first time. (The last time the Cubs were in the World Series, there were no playoffs, just the regular season American League champion versus the regular season National League champion in the World Series.) They then faced the upstart and relatively new Florida Marlins with the right to go to the World Series on the line.

Going into game 6, the Cubs held a 3 games to 2 lead, needing only one more victory to win the series. With one out in the 8th inning and a 3-0 lead, the Cubs were only five outs away from victory when Luis Castillo hit a pop fly into foul territory. Cubs outfielder Moises Alou raced after the fly, leapt up against the barrier and tried to make a play. At the same time, several fans close to the play, Bartman included, reached out to try to catch the ball. Bartman's efforts interfered with Alou, although Bartman failed to catch the ball, and it ended up with another fan while Alou slammed his glove down in frustration.

The Cubs went to the umpire and argued that fan interference occurred and that Castillo should be out, but the umpire disagreed. Once the ball passed the invisible barrier separating the field from the stands, it was fair game for fans. (Two items worth noting here. Firstly, the umpire's call might be incorrect. Replays appear to show that Bartman leans into the field of play where he makes contact with the ball. Second, baseball fans generally know that you try to allow your team's player to make a play on a ball hit by the opposing team even if you have the right to try to catch it because it is coming into the stands. As Bartman is a Cubs fan, he should have tried to allow Alou to make the catch.)

After the incident, the wheels came off for the Cubs. Pitcher Mark Prior walked Castillo, then threw a wild pitch and gave up a single, allowing one run to score. However, the next batter, Miguel Cabrera hit a textbook double play ball that would have ended the inning with the score 3-1, but he booted the play, failing to get any outs. Derrick Lee then doubled to tie the game, Jeff Conine hit a sacrifice fly to take the lead, and Mike Mordecai hit a bases-loaded double. When all was said and done, the score was 8-3, and the game all but lost.

Because of the length of the inning and the controversy, the television broadcast kept cutting to images of Bartman sitting somberly. Fans at Wrigley Field did not initially know who was responsible, but as the inning wore on, they were notified via cell phone by those watching the game on television and they started to turn their ire toward Bartman.

Fans chanted obscenities, threw items at him, and one dumped a cup of beer on his head. Eventually, he needed to be led away by security for his own protection. Almost immediately, Bartman's personal information appeared online. Multiple police cars needed to be parked outside his home, and he changed his phone number to put an end to the threatening calls he was receiving.

In the aftermath, other than issuing an apology and attempting to explain his side of the story, Bartman has kept a low profile. Consistently, he has declined interview requests, endorsement deals, lucrative offers to appear in commercials, and requested that any gifts Marlins fans wanted to send to him be donated to charities.

The Cubs lost game 7 in the series, once more failing to reach the World Series. They would not return until 2016, finally winning in extra innings of game 7.

The actual baseball involved in the incident would be purchased at auction and then detonated in an effort to destroy the curse. Due to multiple reconfigurations of Wrigley Field, Bartman's seat number has been changed multiple times, but the actual seat remains.

When the Cubs won the World Series in 2016, Bartman was sent a championship ring. He has been repeatedly invited back to Wrigley by the Cubs organization, but has refused the request every time.

Answers on the Next Page...

Answers

1) Saddam Hussein
2) Israel
3) Tom from MySpace
4) Heat Wave
5) Land Cruiser War
6) Women
7) Abu Ghraib
8) Ontario
9) North Korea
10) Russia
11) NOC (Non-official cover)
12) MRI (Magnetic Resonance Imaging)
13) Willis McGahee
14) Tesla
15) Mission Accomplished
16) Fred Rogers
17) *The Matrix*
18) Guinea-Bissau
19) Billy Corgan
20) Pijin (Solomon Islands Pidgin)
21) Operation Red Dawn
22) Phil Spector
23) *American Idol*
24) Concorde
25) *Final Fantasy*
26) Arnold Schwarzenegger
27) Curse of the Billy Goat
28) Antwerp
29) Astronomical Unit (AU)
30) Colin Powell

Additional Facts, Fun or Otherwise, from Random Years to Properly Maintain Spacing in this Book

You may have noticed the term Lusophone in one of the previous chapters as we discussed issues in the former Portuguese Empire, a term I was not familiar with until researching this.

Luso as a prefix referring to anything Portuguese goes back to the Roman Empire and the Latin word for Portugal: Lusitania. Which also means that the ship named the *Lusitania* that was sunk in the beginning of World War I was named after the Latin word for Portugal.

Why is this?

The ship's owners, the Cunard Line, frequently named their vessels after Roman provinces. They also built the *Mauretania, Britannia, Caledonia, Hibernia,* and *Cambria.*

In 2004...

1) Five students- Andrew McCollum, Dustin Moskovitz, Chris Hughes, and these two- create a website on the campus of Harvard University. In 18 years, it will have close to 3 billion active users.

2) This planet moves across the face of the sun (from the perspective of we Earth dwellers), appearing as a black dot, a transit which has not occurred since 1882.

3) 193 commuters are killed and thousands are injured in this country during a series of train bombings, which occur three days before the election and may contribute to the Partido Popular party's defeat.

4) Due to no warning systems in the Indian Ocean, residents of coastal areas are taken mostly by surprise by this kind of natural disaster, despite knowing for hours of an undersea earthquake near Indonesia.

5) Construction begins on this building, which will become the tallest in the world. At over half a mile tall, the skyscraper is so high that residents of the upper levels need to wait several more minutes than residents on the lower levels to break their fasts during the month of Ramadan. At the higher level, the sun can be seen for longer before it sets.

6) Rebels stage a coup d'état in this Caribbean nation, although the ousted government will claim without evidence that France and the United States are behind the rebels.

7) At the Summer Olympics in Athens, the shot-put competition is staged in this town, the first Olympics competition held in the town since the 4th century.

8) *Half Life 2* is released to near universal acclaim and will go on to be considered one of the best video games of all time. The main critique against the game is the required usage of this video game distribution service developed by Valve Corporation. It will become the largest distributor of digital games by 2013.

9) Hurricane Catarina makes landfall in Brazil, the first and to date only hurricane to form in this oceanic area.

10) These five central and eastern European countries join both NATO and the European Union.

11) Despite only previously qualifying for two tournaments- the 1980 UEFA European Championship and the 1994 FIFA World Cup- and having never won a game in tournament play, this national soccer team goes on an incredible run, defeating Portugal, drawing Spain, beating France, advancing past the Czech Republic, and shocking hosts Portugal by defeating them a second time to capture the 2004 European Championship.

12) Thieves make away with this Norwegian artist's *Madonna* as well as his most famous piece, both of which are housed in a museum named for the artist. Both pieces will be recovered in 2006 with light damage.

13) This Vermont governor becomes a little too raucous during a speech while campaigning for the Democratic Party nomination for president. The media coverage of his fiery speech quickly turns to mockery, however, and the speech is redubbed the "I Have a Scream" speech.

14) This spacecraft arrives in orbit around Saturn after spending nearly 7 years to get there. It will remain in orbit for thirteen years before burning up in Saturn's atmosphere.

15) This Boston Red Sox outfielder hits two home runs, including a grand slam, in game 7 of the American League Championship Series against the New York Yankees. The Red Sox win 10-3 and become the first baseball team to win a seven game series after being down 3 games to 0.

16) Four contractors working for this company, later renamed Academi, are killed and their bodies are mutilated in Fallujah.

17) The 74 game victory streak on *Jeopardy!* belonging to fellow trivia fanatic and author Ken Jennings comes to an end when he fails to provide this correct response to the answer, "Most of this firm's 70,000 seasonal white-collar employees work only four months a year."

18) This CBS news anchor is publicly shamed and will eventually be forced to resign when it is revealed that documents used in one of

his news reports (specifically those regarding President George Bush's service in the Air National Guard) are forgeries.

19) The Millau Viaduct, the tallest bridge in the world (1100 feet), is opened in this mountain range in southern France.

20) A plan named after this man who served as UN Secretary-General from 1997-2006 brings about a referendum on Cyprus reunification. While the Turkish half of the island votes overwhelmingly in favor, only 24% of the Greek half does.

21) Disgruntled automobile repair shop owner Marvin Heemeyer converts a Komatsu bulldozer into this kind of armored vehicle and uses it to demolish the town hall of Granby, Colorado, a former mayor's house, and several other buildings. He commits suicide rather than be captured when his vehicle becomes stuck in a hardware store.

22) *Lord of the Rings: The Return of the King* wins a historic and record tying 11 Academy Awards (tied with *Ben-Hur* and *Titanic*) in a clean sweep of nominated categories, despite not receiving any nominations or awards in this group of categories.

23) IBM sells its Personal Computer business to this Chinese company, making it the third largest provider of PCs after Dell and Hewlett-Packard.

24) This former NFL football player, who gave up his lucrative pro football career to join the military after 9/11, is killed in Iraq. The military will initially claim that he was killed by enemy combatants, but eventually will admit he was killed by friendly fire.

25) NASA's X-43A, this kind of jet using supersonic compression and exhaust, achieves Mach 9.6 or close to 6700 miles per hour.

26) A British artist creates spoofs of British 10 pound bank notes, removing Queen Elizabeth II's image and replacing it with one of Princess Diana. The text on the bills was also changed from the "Bank of England" to this appropriate expression.

27) In the fallout from controversy surrounding the Super Bowl halftime show, with Justin Timberlake ripping off part of Jessica Jackson's dress, this two word phrase is coined to explain the incident, despite the stunt being intentional.

28) Wangari Maathai, founder of this Kenyan environmental and women's empowerment movement, is awarded the Nobel Peace Prize.

29) An expedition from Ukraine descends into a new chamber in the Krubera Cave, more than 2000 meters below the surface. This is the first time in the history of this discipline that a team has broken the 2000 meter threshold.

30) A fight breaks out between fans of this basketball team and players after a fan throws a cup at Indiana Pacers forward Ron Artest. Because the name of the arena is the Palace in Auburn Hills, the brawl becomes known as the Malice at the Palace.

Random Fact, Fun or Otherwise

Coming into the 2004 Presidential campaigning season in the United States (which actually began in 2003), Howard Dean had a bit of momentum. As a former governor of Vermont, he- unlike most of his Democratic opponents- had not been in the federal government and had not cast a vote in favor of the war in Iraq. The war was highly popular when declared initially, but had fast been losing ground. With his anti-war stance, and his left-wing populist style, Dean was positioning himself to capture the working-class left, the anti-war left, and the anti-corporate left portions of the party.

However, prior to his infamous speech, the wheels were already coming off the Dean campaign. Poor campaign organization led to poor voter outreach, poor utilization of resources, and poor execution of campaign strategy. The energy Dean brought to his speeches led some to perceive him as somewhat unhinged, and this was before the speech that came to define his political career.

After finishing third in the Iowa Caucus, the first state to vote in the nomination process, supporters were saddened, but still excited to meet their candidate. Wanting to recapture some momentum and perhaps some national attention, Dean walked out on the stage like a rock star as the crowd roared. After taking off his jacket and rolling up his sleeves, he exhorted the crowd to keep fighting, culminating with, "Not only are we going to New Hampshire, Tom Harkin, we're going to South Carolina and Oklahoma and Arizona and North Dakota and New Mexico, and we're going to California and Texas and New York. And we're going to South Dakota and Oregon and Washington and Michigan, and then we're going to Washington, D.C., to take back the White House! YEAH!"

The moment was played 633 times in national news over the next 4 days. Reporters present for the event did not find the rally to be anything unusual. What is jarring however for the television viewer is that their feed came strictly from the microphone Dean was holding, which was naturally capturing him in full throat and not so much the roaring crowd in the background. The audio helped to give the impression that Dean was having some kind of breakdown on the stage when watched on television.

The clip became one of the first viral Internet memes, and the moment was fodder for late night talk show hosts. Politicos of the time blamed the gaffe for Dean's subsequent defeat in the New Hampshire primary, however, pundits now do not see where Dean's campaign could have gone forward regardless.

In addition to comic fodder, the scream has been used by additional politicians, turned into dance music, and even by Dean himself when he made a parody while campaigning against Chris Christie. Perhaps in one hundred years' time, it will have replaced the Wilhelm Scream.

Answers on the Next Page...

Answers

1) Mark Zuckerberg & Eduardo Saverin
2) Venus
3) Spain
4) Tsunami
5) Burj Khalifa
6) Haiti
7) Olympia
8) Steam
9) Southern Atlantic Ocean
10) Slovakia, Slovenia, Latvia, Lithuania, & Estonia
11) Greece
12) Edvard Munch (The other stolen piece was *The Scream.*)
13) Howard Dean
14) *Cassini (Cassini-Huygens)*
15) Johnny Damon
16) Blackwater
17) "What is H&R Block?"
18) Dan Rather
19) Massif Central
20) Kofi Annan
21) Tank
22) Acting
23) Lenovo
24) Pat Tillman
25) Scramjet
26) "Banksy of England"
27) Wardrobe malfunction
28) Green Belt Movement
29) Speleology
30) Detroit Pistons

Additional Facts, Fun or Otherwise, from Random Years to Properly Maintain Spacing in this Book

I know what you're thinking- you just made reference to a Wilhelm scream, and I have no idea what that is. And yet, if you have ever seen a movie, you probably do; you just don't know it.

The Wilhelm scream is a stock sound effect believed to be performed by Sheb Wooley, an actor and singer perhaps best known for performing the song, "The Purple People Eater." As a background actor on the 1951 film *Distant Drums*, Wooley and others recorded screams to be used when their characters marched through an alligator-infested swamp. Officially, the sound clip is called, "Man getting bit by an alligator, and he screams." It was used in multiple Warner Brothers films in the 1950s and 1960s.

The scream became iconic when sound designer Ben Burtt used the scream in *Star Wars* as a stormtrooper is shot and falls from a height. Burtt named the scream after the character of Private Wilhem in the 1953 film *The Charge at Feather River*. The scream is used when Wilhelm is shot in the thigh with an arrow.

The scream appears in every *Star Wars* and *Indiana Jones* franchise film, as well as in every subsequent film Ben Burtt has worked on. It has also appeared in dozens if not hundreds of other movies, television shows, and even video games.

In 2005...

1) This massive structure in New Orleans, the shelter of last resort for natural disasters in the area, becomes a symbol of the destruction wrought by Hurricane Katrina. Thousands of people ride out the storm there, the building receives considerable damage, and there are reports of gang activity, drug dealing, and violence within.

2) Rafiq Hariri, former prime minister of this country, credited with shepherding the country out of civil war, is assassinated by a suicidal bomber in a truck. Both Hezbollah and Syrian occupying forces will be blamed.

3) A team led by Michael Brown at Palomar Observatory discovers this dwarf planet, second largest in the solar system. It will later be named after the Greek goddess of strife and discord.

4) "Meet Me at the Zoo" becomes the first video on this website.

5) This comedian and actor takes over hosting duties on the *Late Late Show*, the first non-American to host an American late night talk show.

6) After 15 years in a vegetative state, this woman whose case has been argued in multiple courts and the media, including between President Bush and right-to-die advocates, is removed from life support and allowed to die.

7) The A830, the first double decker air liner, makes its maiden flight from Toulouse, corporate home of this aviation company.

8) The National Symphony Orchestra under the baton of Leonard Slatkin premiers this composer's 7th symphony with the composer in attendance. The piece is also known as the *Toltec Symphony*.

9) Israel destroys all Israeli settlements and withdraws all forces from this territory. Many will still consider the land illegally occupied by Israeli forces.

10) This cyclist wins his record-setting seventh straight Tour de France. All his victories will later be vacated.

11) At Six Flags Great America, Kinda Ka briefly becomes the fastest and tallest roller coaster in the world. By featuring a drop of more than 400 feet, it is officially classified as this kind of coaster.

12) The first in a series of Christian allegorical novels by this British author is adapted into a film, directed by Andrew Adamson. It will finish the year with the third highest grossing box office of the year.

13) Falschermuseum opens in Vienna, a museum dedicated to this type of art.

14) In July, this organization officially ends its military campaign and drops its arms in compliance with the 1998 Good Friday Agreement.

15) After being cancelled in 2002, this cartoon returns to Fox's Sunday night, given a second chance due to the popularity of its reruns on Cartoon Network.

16) This member of the Christian Democratic Union party becomes chancellor of Germany, the first woman to hold the office.

17) The project known as GIMPS- the Great Internet these Search- finds the forty-third example of their quarry.

18) This British playwright of the *Birthday Party* and *Betrayal* wins the Nobel Prize for Literature.

19) During *A Concert for Hurricane Relief* broadcast on NBC, this musician makes the statement, "George Bush doesn't care about black people."

20) This actress, only three years removed from winning an Oscar for *Monster's Ball*, wins a Golden Raspberry (Razzie) for worst actor. She shows to receive the award in person and give a thank you speech.

21) Danish newspaper *Jyllands-Posten* controversially publishes several cartoons featuring this figure, causing outrage throughout the world.

22) This American tennis player, a three-time major champion and an Olympic gold medal winner, has a rough year at the hands of the Williams sisters, losing the Australian Open final to Serena and the Wimbledon final to Venus.

23) After being mauled, Isabelle Dinoire becomes the first person to receive this kind of transplant.

24) Chad devolves into civil war with Sudan-supported fighters attacking this capital city.

25) This word, which technically describes what tweeting is, is introduced into the English language.
26) This Canadian actor, famous for playing a Scotsman on American television, dies at the age of 85. His ashes will be spread in space.
27) The first entry in this video game series is released with a replica Gibson SG.
28) FBI agent Mark Felt reveals he is the source of reporter Bob Woodward nicknamed this.

𝕽𝖆𝖓𝖉𝖔𝖒 𝕱𝖆𝖈𝖙, 𝕱𝖚𝖓 𝖔𝖗 𝕺𝖙𝖍𝖊𝖗𝖜𝖎𝖘𝖊

The battle between Jay Leno and David Letterman to take over the *Tonight Show* is often called The Late Night Wars, so what happened in 2004 and 2005 was perhaps the first shots in a war that might be called a succession crisis. The 12:30 slot was dominated by Conan O'Brien, more of a comedy writer than a comedian, but who had a unique style and a dedicated fan base in a desirable demographic.

CBS's offering at the time was Craig Kilbourn, maybe the only man in television history who has twice left a show and each time replaced with a host widely considered a huge upgrade. (He had previously given up the desk at *The Daily Show*, handing the reins to Jon Stewart.) The fact that you're probably wondering what happened to Craig Kilbourn- if you even recognize his name at all- tells you what kind of impact he had on the national zeitgeist.

Back in 2001, with Conan's popularity, he was seen as the heir apparent to Leno's seat, but the situation was perhaps more urgent than that. Other networks were courting Conan for new 11:30 slots to rival *The Tonight Show*, and Conan was ready to move up an hour. NBC decided to make it official that Conan would take over in 2009. However, they neglected to tell Leno until 2004.

It seemed like a good idea at the time. One thing they did not factor was Craig Ferguson.

Here is where the section of Random Fact departs into Random Supposition, otherwise known as the Ministry of Trivia's opinion. We would point out that Jay Leno concurred with our assessment in a recent interview. Eight years is a long time in television, a long time to hold a job in wait for anyone, because anything can happen.

Craig Ferguson's take on the late-night talk show was innovative, deconstructionist, and a little odd, but like Conan before him, it earned him an extraordinarily dedicated fan base. His improv-heavy monologues, the use of a robotic skeleton (voiced by Josh Robert Thompson) as a sidekick, and his eclectic interview style (featuring him grandiosely tearing up the info sheet his research team had provided him for each guest) stood in stark contrast to Conan, who suddenly seemed more stilted.

Ferguson began to pass Conan in the ratings in 2007, while Conan did not move as mainstream as NBC executives hoped he might. Meanwhile, Leno continued to post solid ratings for NBC, and there were talks that Leno might move to Fox or ABC, competing directly against Conan.

In a desperate move that a lot of executives in private thought would fail, NBC decided to move Conan to *The Tonight Show* and give Leno a new show at the 10:00 timeslot. After a successful first week, ratings began to plummet for both new shows.

With network affiliates threatening to preempt Jay Leno's show by running syndicated shows or the news earlier, NBC scrambled to fix the situation. The initial thought was to move Jay Leno to 11:30, trim his show to thirty minutes, and then have *The Tonight Show* begin at midnight. While Leno was receptive to this idea, Conan was not, and shortly into the process, made the announcement that he would be leaving *The Tonight Show*.

Jay Leno resumed hosting duties in 2010, and he led *The Tonight Show* until 2014. After a stipulated, contractual amount of time off air, Conan went to TBS. Craig Ferguson continued to host *The Late Late Show* until 2014, when he went through a much smaller succession crisis of his own when Stephen Colbert was selected to take over for David Letterman.

Answers on the Next Page...

Answers

1) Superdome
2) Lebanon
3) Eris
4) YouTube
5) Craig Ferguson
6) Terry Schiavo
7) Airbus
8) Phillip Glass
9) Gaza Strip
10) Lance Armstrong
11) Strato Coaster
12) C.S. Lewis
13) Forgeries
14) Irish Republican Army
15) *Family Guy*
16) Angela Merkel
17) Mersenne Prime
18) Harold Pinter
19) Kanye West
20) Halle Berry
21) Muhammad
22) Lindsay Davenport
23) Face transplant
24) N'Djamena
25) Microblogging
26) James Doohan
27) *Guitar Hero*
28) Deep Throat

𝕴𝖓 2006...

1) This national women's ice hockey team upsets the United States in the semifinals at the Olympics ensuring that for the first time the women's ice hockey gold medal match will not be the United States vs Canada.

2) This planet receives a demotion after the International Astronomical Union redefines the definition of a planet.

3) Twitter, now X, is co-founded by this man who serves as its first CEO.

4) Seven explosives- all this kind of improvised explosive device (IED)- detonate within 11 minutes of each other in Mumbai's railway system.

5) With 55.5% of the populace voting yes, this country with a capital city of Podgorica barely clears the 55% required threshold on the referendum for independence.

6) Nearly 400 pilgrims are killed in Mecca during a stampede occurring during the last day of this annual five-day event.

7) This game platform created by David Baszucki and Erik Cassel is released, but will not begin to gain massive popularity until the late 2010s.

8) The Metropolitan Police Service in the United Kingdom discovers a plot to smuggle explosives on board transatlantic air flights in these, which leads to increased security measure around the amount of liquid passengers are allowed to bring on board a plane.

9) This artist's painting *No. 5, 1948* sets a record for highest amount spent for a painting at $140 million.

10) At the 2006 FIFA World Cup, a round of 16 match between Portugal and the Netherlands features a total 16 yellow cards and 4 red cards, with 2 players being sent off for each team. It will become known as the Battle of this Bavarian German city, unofficially the capital of Franconia.

11) The bombing of the al-Askari shrine in Samarra, a holy site to this sect of Islam, leads to sectarian violence in Iraq.

12) This Prime Minister of the United Kingdom, losing popularity due to his support of the War in Iraq, agrees to resign. His resignation will take place in 2007.

13) Merchant vessel *Probo Koala* offloads toxic waste in Abidjan, a city in this country, leading to thousands of cases of poisoning and several deaths.

14) This president of Mexico orders the military to begin combatting drug cartels, opening a new theatre in the War on Drugs.

15) The Nobel Prize in Peace goes to Muhammad Yunus of Bangladesh and his company Grameen Bank, which pioneered the use of this kind of financing in impoverished areas.

16) This film released in late 2005 from director Ang Lee takes a step forward in the representation of homosexuality in Hollywood films and wins Lee the Best Director Oscar at the Academy Awards.

17) Ben Bernanke is appointed to this position, sometimes called the second most powerful man in the world.

18) This sculpture by Anish Kapoor, officially called Cloud Gate, is completed in AT&T Plaza in Millennium Park in Chicago. Chicago residents generally refer to the sculpture as this.

19) Lawyer Harry Whittington receives his 15 minutes of fame as the victim of an accidental shooting at the hands of this man.

20) The single "Who Says You Can't Go Home" from this New Jersey-based band goes to number 1 on the U.S. Hot Country charts, becoming the first song from a rock band to top a country chart.

21) In the first game back in the Superdome after Hurricane Katrina, the New Orleans Saints defeat their archrival Atlanta Falcons 23-3. The iconic image from the game- Steve Gleason's flying punt block which was recovered for a touchdown- will be made into a statue entitled *Rebirth* after it is revealed Gleason is fighting this disease which also afflicted Lou Gehrig.

22) While filming underwater for a documentary on the Great Barrier Reef, this star of "The Crocodile Hunter" is killed by the barbed tail of a stingray.

23) Three players from this university's lacrosse team are accused of sexual assault and rape by an exotic dancer. They will eventually be cleared, and the D.A. forced to resign over allegations of prosecutorial misconduct, but not before the trial is waged extensively in the media.

24) This Sacramento, California based franchise music store, which expanded rapidly in the 1990s, falls prey to the curse of the Internet and files for bankruptcy.

25) The CW Network emerges out of the merger of these two television networks.

26) In what is widely considered one of the greatest college football games of all time, this Texas Longhorns quarterback scrambles for a 9-yard touchdown run on 4th down with nineteen seconds remaining to defeat the USC Trojans in the national championship game.

27) The release of this movie, the second highest grossing film of the year, spurs protest from religious groups- especially Catholic groups- as well as from the National Organization for Albinism and Hypopigmentation.

28) This newly released 7th Generation video game console reinvigorates Nintendo's position in the console industry.

29) A newly discovered tree of this species found on the Pacific coast of North America, which will be named Hyperion, is determined to be the tallest tree in the world at 380 feet.

30) This game show host announces that the current season of *The Price is Right* will be his last, ending his 35-year run.

Random Fact, Fun or Otherwise

The 2006 World Cup shattered records for the most yellow and red cards handed out during a World Cup. Much of the blame has been placed at the feet of FIFA President Sepp Blatter, who wanted referees to call games more tightly. 345 yellow cards and 28 red cards were handed out across 112 games, leading to widespread suspensions of players for advancing teams (due to yellow card accumulation or receiving red cards).

In the round of 16 match between the Netherlands and Portugal, Russian referee Valentin Ivanov handed out 16 yellow cards, four of which were second yellows, thereby becoming red cards. Despite these attempts at discipline, the game did escape from the referee in the second half and animosity rose between the two teams.

During a melee near the touchline, Portuguese star Figo headbutted Dutchman Mark van Bommel. Another melee was started when Khalid Boulahrouz fouled Figo, earning a second yellow and a sending off. Then Portuguese midfielder Deco harshly fouled John Heitinga in response to the Dutch refusing to concede possession after Portugal had played the ball into touch to allow an injured Dutch player to receive treatment (as is the normal practice).

Portugal advanced to the quarterfinals and then the semifinals, each time playing without two of their starters due to suspensions. The 2006 World Cup is at least partially responsible for changes to how FIFA carries forward yellow cards against players in future World Cups.

Answers on the Next Page...

Answers

1) Sweden
2) Pluto
3) Jack Dorsey
4) Pressure cooker bomb
5) Montenegro
6) Hajj
7) Roblox
8) Soda cans
9) Jackson Pollack
10) Nuremburg
11) Shi'a (Shi'ite)
12) Tony Blair
13) Cote d'Ivoire (Ivory Coast)
14) Felipe Calderon
15) Microcredit (Microloans)
16) *Brokeback Mountain*
17) Chairman of the Federal Reserve of the United States
18) "The Bean"
19) Dick Cheney
20) Bon Jovi
21) ALS (amyotrophic lateral sclerosis)
22) Steve Irwin
23) Duke University
24) Tower Records
25) The WB (Warner Brothers) and UPN (United Paramount Network)
26) Vince Young
27) *The Da Vinci Code*
28) Nintendo Wii
29) Redwood
30) Bob Barker

Additional Facts, Fun or Otherwise, from Random Years to Properly Maintain Spacing in this Book

The Great Internet Mersenne Prime Search is a collaborative volunteer effort to find Mersenne Prime numbers. Volunteers download software and donate their systems' computing power to run algorithms that attempt to find Mersenne Primes.

What is a Mersenne Prime you ask…?

A Mersenne Prime is a prime number (only divisible by the integers 1 and itself) which conforms to the following formula: 2^n-1. For example, 3 is a Mersenne Prime ($2^2-1=3$) as is 7 ($2^3-1=7$), but 5 is not, despite being a prime as well. In fact, it is known that for this equation to work, the exponent n in 2^n-1 must also be a prime number.

What is the importance or relevance of a Mersenne Prime you ask…?

(pause for dramatic effect)

Officially, the Ministry of Trivia has no idea. We're trivia nerds, not math nerds.

In 2007...

1) This two-time Prime Minister of Pakistan and current leader of the opposition is assassinated when her SUV is attacked by gunfire and suicide bombers.

2) After 18 years on the small screen, this cartoon family of five makes their big screen debut.

3) In order to deal with insurgencies in Iraq, the U.S. government decides to ramp up the number of troops in country under the operational title New Way Forward. In the media, however, it was generally referred to as this.

4) The housing bubble pops, and a financial crisis is prompted because of many of these higher risk loans defaulting.

5) Off-duty police officers are hired to guard AT&T retail stores in anticipation of the release of this smartphone, retailing for $499. In 2023, an unopened first edition model will sell at auction for $190,000.

6) This Congresswoman from the Democratic Party becomes the first woman to be elected by her peers to the position of Speaker of the House.

7) The Russian military opens fire on Georgian forces in the Kodori Valley, the only part of this breakaway Georgian republic that is under central government control.

8) This novel, the final in a seven-book series, sets records by selling 11 million copies in the first 24 hours of release. (Side note: The Ministry of Trivia closed for this day, so the Minister could read all 784 pages in one day.)

9) The World Cup of this sport is held in the West Indies for the first time, appropriate as the West Indies are the two-time winners. However, in this iteration, Australia emerges victorious.

10) Sheikh Mohammad bin Rashid Al Maktoum, ruler of this city and prime minister of the United Arab Emirates, makes the largest single charitable donation ever of over 7 billion euros to his educational foundation.

11) Yue Minjun's 1995 painting *Execution,* a commentary on this 1989 event, sells at Sotheby's for $5.9 million, the most ever for a contemporary Chinese artist.

12) Operation Banner officially comes to an end for the British Armed Forces as they withdraw from this location, ending the longest continuous military deployment in British history.

13) Five Belgian nurses and one doctor are freed from prison in this country after being falsely accused of deliberately infecting hospitalized children with HIV and having their confessions tortured out of them.

14) This San Francisco Giants slugger hits his 756th home run of his career, passing Hank Aaron for most home runs in a career. The achievement will be partially overshadowed by allegations of the use of performance enhancing drugs.

15) Along with the Intergovernmental Panel on Climate Change, this former American politician wins the Nobel Peace Prize to go with a future Grammy, an Emmy, and a prominent role in an Academy Award winning documentary.

16) This NBA referee turns himself into the FBI after an investigation reveals that he has been gambling on games he refereed.

17) On its first day of release, this video game, made exclusively for Xbox 360 and featuring the lead character Master Chief, makes $170 million in sales. Over the course of the first week, it will make $300 million, and it will sell 14.5 million copies.

18) This website, founded by Julian Assange, reveals a document entitled *Standard Operating Procedures for Camp Delta,* a U.S. military handbook for dealing with prisoners at Guantanamo Bay. The guide specifies how to evade protocols of the Geneva Convention.

19) Riots break out in this former Soviet republic as the government orders the removal of the Bronze Soldier of Tallinn, a World War II monument seen by some as emblematic of Soviet rule.

20) This radio personality is fired from his eponymous talk show after making several racially insensitive comments about the players for the Rutgers University women's basketball team.

21) Per this amendment to the American constitution, Vice-president Dick Cheney becomes Acting President of the United States while George Bush is under anesthesia for a colonoscopy procedure.

22) With Operation Outside the Box, Israeli F-15s and F-16s cross the border into this country's airspace and strike a site believed to be an undeclared nuclear reactor. The International Atomic Energy Agency will investigate the site later and find evidence of uranium.

23) The series finale of this HBO drama ends seemingly in the middle of a scene at a diner. As the door to the diner opens, the screen cuts to black, leaves several moments of silence, and then rolls credits.

24) In one of college football's great upsets, this university team from Boone, North Carolina becomes the first FCS (Football Championship Subdivision, formerly division I-AA) team to defeat a ranked FBS team (Football Bowl Subdivision, formerly division I). A last second blocked field goal preserves a 34-32 victory against the #5 University of Michigan Wolverines.

25) This darkly humorous American author succumbs to injuries sustained in a fall and passes away at the age of 84, one year after joking he should sue cigarette manufacturers (because the labels on the cigarettes promised that they would kill him faster). His son will release an unpublished collection of stories and essays *Armageddon in Retrospect* almost ten years after his most recently published fiction *God Bless You, Dr. Kevorkian* (1999) and *Timequake* (1997).

26) A viral marketing prank for this television show causes a bomb panic in Boston when battery-powered LED signs depicting Mooninites are found in the city and the surrounding towns.

27) Professional wrestling star Chris Benoit murders his wife and son and then commits suicide. Medical examinations of his brain indicate that the amount of damage done is similar to that of an elderly Alzheimer's patient and that Benoit was likely suffering from severe dementia associated with this condition, often associated with athletes and head injuries.

28) The US House of Representatives passes this act, named for a victim of homophobia-related torture and murder, the first gay rights bill brought to the floor for a vote. The bill will die in the Senate, but will be made law in 2009.

29) A bridge over this river on I-35 in Minnesota collapses, killing 13 and injuring over 100.

Random Fact, Fun or Otherwise

The 2007 Michigan Wolverines were favorites to win the Big Ten Conference and possibly contend for a national championship, as they came into their "tune-up" game against FCS Appalachian State. ASU was no slouch in their division, however, having won back-to-back national titles in the lower-level league.

Michigan's defeat had some wide-ranging implications and lasting legacy. The loss dropped them out of the top 25 rankings, the first time ever a team ranked that highly had fallen completely out of the rankings. The Associated Press, responsible for creating the top 25, amended their policy to allow FCS teams to be considered in the FBS poll. After ASU finished their season 13-2 with a third straight national championship, they became the first FCS team to receive votes in the FBS poll, placing them in 34th place (out of approximately 110 FBS teams).

Michigan's defeat was not the only loss of impressive proportions in the 2007 college football year. The University of Notre Dame, referred to as "The University of Football in America" by at least one prominent sportswriter, lost in triple overtime, 46-44, to the United States Naval Academy. The Midshipmen had not defeated the Fighting Irish since 1963 and had gone 0-43 in that time against Notre Dame. It was the longest win streak for one college football team against another.

Answers on the Next Page...

Answers

1) Benazir Bhutto
2) The Simpsons
3) The Surge
4) Subprime mortgages
5) iPhone
6) Nancy Pelosi
7) Abkhazia
8) *Harry Potter and the Deathly Hallows*
9) Cricket
10) Dubai
11) Tiananmen Square
12) Northern Ireland
13) Libya
14) Barry Bonds
15) Al Gore
16) Tim Donaghy
17) *Halo 3*
18) WikiLeaks
19) Estonia
20) Don Imus
21) 25th Amendment
22) Syria
23) *The Sopranos*
24) Appalachian State University Mountaineers
25) Kurt Vonnegut
26) *Aqua Teen Hunger Force*
27) Chronic Traumatic Encephalopathy (CTE)
28) Matthew Shephard Act
29) Mississippi River

In 2008…

1) The Church of Scientology finds itself under cyber assault from this "hacktivist" group after the Church sues YouTube for copyright infringement over a leaked interview with Tom Cruise.

2) This film serves as the inspiration for the introduction of a synonym in American English for "to jump the shark" in the form of "to nuke the fridge."

3) Financial markets plummet as this event, begun the year prior with the collapse in the housing market, jumps into overdrive.

4) At the 2008 Summer Olympics, the cycling event's course passes through this man-made structure that once demarcated the northern border of Imperial China.

5) This Himalayan kingdom transitions from absolute monarchy to a parliamentary system following the ratification of a new constitution.

6) *The Hunger Games*, from this author of *Gregor the Overlander*, is released to critical acclaim.

7) Canadian Prime Minister Stephen Harper apologies to First Nations peoples for this system, which attempted to remove indigenous children's cultural heritage and assimilate them into Canadian society.

8) The election of Barack Obama provides many firsts, including the first American president to have been born in this state.

9) In a white paper published under the pseudonym of Satoshi Nakamoto, a to-this-day unknown author describes the beginning designs of this cryptocurrency and the creation of its blockchain database.

10) After the death of this comedian, NBC reruns the first episode of *Saturday Night Live*, which was hosted by the aforementioned comedian.

11) An avalanche in an area of this mountain known as "The Bottleneck" kills eleven mountaineers, the deadliest incident on the mountain in climbing history.

12) This fourth largest investment bank in the United States, originally founded in 1847, goes bankrupt.

13) For the first since the 0-14 1976 Tampa Bay Buccaneers, an NFL teams loses all of its games. This team experiences slightly greater ignominy as they go 0-16. The feat will be duplicated by the 2017 Cleveland Browns.

14) The United States Navy destroys one of these (an outdated American one) with a missile, leading to speculation that the military is attempting to develop the ability to destroy those of rival countries.

15) Margaret Atwood, perhaps best known for this novel adapted into an Emmy award winning Hulu series, pens the non-fiction work *Payback: Debt and the Shadow Side of Wealth*.

16) This particle accelerator built by CERN near Geneva goes online.

17) Elliot Spitzer, governor of this state, is forced to resign after revelations that he has been using a high-priced prostitution service come to light.

18) This musician/actor who won an Academy Award for the theme music to *Shaft*, starred in a John Carpenter film, and voiced Chef on *South Park* dies of a stroke at the age of 65.

19) Journalist Muntadhar al-Zaidi makes news of his own, throwing these at President George Bush during a press conference in Iraq.

20) In a rare example of a sequel improving upon its progenitor, this film from Christopher Nolan receives near universal acclaim on its way to becoming the highest grossing film of the year.

21) This governor of Illinois is arrested on corruption charges from his attempts to sell the vacated Senate seat of president-elect Obama.

22) With a chance to clinch victory during a penalty kick shootout which would decide the UEFA Champions League final, this Chelsea captain slips on the grass and puts his penalty off the post. Manchester United goalkeeper Edwin van der Sar subsequently saves Nicholas Anelka's attempt and United win the shootout, 6-5.

23) The U.S. Department of the Interior lists this animal as endangered due to the effect of melting Arctic sea ice.

24) Two new notes- an A flat and a C- are depressed on an organ in Halberstadt, Germany, the fourth chord to be played since 2001

as part of a 639-year plan to play this composer's *Organ2 ASLSP* (*As Slow As Possible*).

25) The isle of Salk, a Channel Island and part of the Bailiwick of Guernsey, becomes the last European country to ban this medieval system.

26) The NHL All-Star Game is held in this city, which has twice held NHL franchises, but has never kept one. The former Atlanta teams are now the Calgary Flames and the new incarnation of the Winnipeg Jets.

27) Cincinnati television station WBQC receives permission to change their call letters to this appropriate call sign.

28) Investment manager Bernie Madoff is arrested on charges of fraud. It will be revealed that he has been running the largest example of this kind of scheme in history.

29) The premier of this film from director Jon Favreau begins a new "universe" and a race for other entertainment properties to do the same.

30) At the 2008 U.S. Open, Tiger Woods overcomes a leg injury and defeats this golfer in an 18-hole playoff to capture his 14th major title. It will be his last until the 2019 Masters.

𝕽𝖆𝖓𝖉𝖔𝖒 𝕱𝖆𝖈𝖙, 𝕱𝖚𝖓 𝖔𝖗 𝕺𝖙𝖍𝖊𝖗𝖜𝖎𝖘𝖊

The creation of the Marvel Cinematic Universe is certainly a landmark in the history of film. While sequels and continuations have existed for a long time, the idea of telling film stories in comic book form (i.e. several stand-alone stories with some interconnection, shared plotlines, and ramification on the greater story combined with team-up releases) is novel, it is not the first instance of a shared universe cropping up in film.

In some cases, these are one-off references or overlapping crossover characters, such as in the Quentin Tarantino verse (no official name) or in films and television shows based on the works of Elmore Leonard (where characters like Ray Nicolette or Karen Sisco crop up multiple times.) Or they can be a little more in-depth where characters cross over, having multiple plot impacts, or engage in team-ups, such as in the View Askewniverse from Kevin Smith (with *Jay and Silent Bob Strike Back* being their "Avengers.") Others- like the Matrix Universe- have the full film storyline flushed out by additional media, such as cartoons or video games. There are even examples from classic cinema, such as the Universal Monster movies or the Toho *Godzilla* franchise which might be considered cinematic universes.

In television, it is far more common, even though we do not tend to think of these shows as shared universes but rather as spinoffs. *Cheers* launched multiple spinoffs, but also had crossovers with other NBC comedies. *Buffy the Vampire Slayer*, *The X-Files*, *Stargate*, *Xena: Warrior Princess*, *CSI*, Shondaland, *Breaking Bad*, *The Vampire Diaries*, *The Walking Dead*, *Arrow*, *The Cosby Show*, and the Dick Wolf entertainment empire are all examples of shared universes.

Of course, with the Marvel Cinematic Universe striking it rich and seemingly having unlocked some kind of cheat code which allows an essential license to print money, every other studio has attempted to create their own film universes. Two different Marvel-related comic book universes have been folded into or are shared with the MCU, these being the Fox *X-Men* film series and the Sony owned *Spider-man* series. Marvel's great comic book rival, DC, has created their own film universe (which somewhat runs in competition with the DC-based Arrowverse on the CW).

Star Wars, *The Lord of the Rings*, *The Fast & The Furious*, and the Wizarding World of Harry Potter have all expanded beyond their initial storylines to include more "in-universe" stories with varying degrees of success. The two most successful new universes to rival the MCU might be the MonsterVerse, featuring Godzilla and King Kong related films; and the Conjuring Universe, which now stands as the highest grossing horror film franchise.

Answers on the Next Page...

𝕬𝕹𝕾𝕸𝖊𝖗𝖘

1) Anonymous
2) *Indiana Jones and the Kingdom of the Crystal Skull*
3) Great Recession
4) Great Wall of China
5) Bhutan
6) Stephanie Collins
7) Canadian Indian Residential School System
8) Hawaii
9) Bitcoin
10) George Carlin
11) K2
12) Lehman Brothers
13) Detroit Lions
14) Satellite
15) *The Handmaid's Tale*
16) Large Hadron Collider
17) New York
18) Isaac Hayes
19) His shoes
20) *Dark Knight*
21) Rod Blagojevich
22) John Terry
23) Polar bear
24) John Cage
25) Feudalism
26) Atlanta
27) WKRP
28) Ponzi Scheme
29) *Iron Man*
30) Rocco Mediate

𝕴𝖓 2009…

1) US Airways Flight 1549 strikes birds and loses both engines while taking off from LaGuardia Airport in New York City. Pilot Chesley Sullenberger successfully ditches the aircraft in this body of water, and the entire complement of passengers and crew are rescued.

2) Singer Michael Jackson is found dead from an overdose of this drug, an anesthetic dubbed "milk of amnesia."

3) This film also directed by James Cameron surpasses *Titanic* as the highest grossing film of all time.

4) Twenty thousand people around the globe are diagnostically confirmed and an additional 275,000 are estimated to have been killed by the H1N1 pandemic, better known as this.

5) Israel withdraws from the Gaza Strip after a ceasefire agreement is brokered between Israel and Hamas. Rockets will continue to be launched from the Gaza Strip, spurring the need for this Israeli defensive system, which will be implemented in 2011.

6) The United States defeats this national soccer team, the reigning European champion, 2-0, in the semifinals of the 2009 Confederation Cup, snapping their 35-game unbeaten streak. The Americans' defeated opponent will go on to win the 2010 World Cup and the 2012 European championship.

7) At this American university, still coming to grips with a mass shooting event from two years previous, Chinese student Zhu Haiyang murders fellow student Yang Xin via decapitation, allegedly for spurning his romantic advances.

8) The 12th installment of this fantasy series is released, written by Brandon Sanderson from notes left by Robert Jordan.

9) Inflation in this island nation and banking hub reaches 18.6% as the Great Recession decimates its banking sector.

10) The Kepler space telescope is placed into orbit to search for exoplanets, by the use of this instrument that specifically measures the brightness of stars, while searching for dimming that might indicate planets.

11) Protests break out in major cities across Iran as this politician declares victory in his reelection campaign despite reports of voting irregularities.

12) This Australian actor makes his film debut playing the executive officer of the *USS Kelvin* and the father of James Tiberius Kirk, while his brother makes his debut in the Nicolas Cage vehicle *Knowing*.

13) Omar al-Bashir, the president of this country, becomes the first sitting governmental leader to be charged by the International Criminal Court. The charges include war crimes and genocide.

14) This online video game, published by Riot Games, becomes available to play. The game will become the world's largest e-sport, with the 2019 event drawing in 100 million viewers.

15) Entering the English lexicon is this hyphenated term, referring to far-right, white nationalism, especially in the United State. The origin of the term is credited to the website 4chan.

16) This 20-year-old British singer receives the best new artist award at the Grammys.

17) Six-year-old Falcon Heene is dubbed this by the media after his parents stage a hoax capturing national attention and necessitating a frantic deployment of National Guard air assets.

18) This Islamist terrorist group begins an uprising in Nigeria, but Nigerian forces put down the group quickly. Approximately 1,000 civilians are killed in under a week.

19) The television series *ER*, created by this medical doctor and novelist, signs off after 331 episodes.

20) Despite being granted home rule by Denmark in 1979, this island implements self-rule, which is seen as a potential step toward eventual independence.

21) Notorious spree killer John Allen Muhammad, better known by this moniker, has his final plea for clemency denied and he is executed via lethal injection.

22) The fifth novel in the *Percy Jackson and the Olympians* series by this author reaches the top of the New York Times Best Sellers List.

23) Captain Richard Phillips of this vessel is taken captive by Somali pirates and held hostage until a U.S. Navy Seal team assaults the

lifeboat in which he is held, killing the pirates and rescuing Phillips.

24) At Wimbledon, Roger Federer and this American play a lengthy five set final with Federer winning the final set and the match, 16-14.

25) This former judge for the U.S. District Court for the Southern District of New York is confirmed as a Supreme Court Justice, becoming the third woman, the first woman of color, and the first person of Hispanic descent in the Supreme Court.

26) *The Newlywed Game* features a gay couple for the first time in the form of Brad Altman and this actor currently playing the recurring role as Kaito Nakamura on the show *Heroes*.

27) Under Executive Order 13505, President Obama removes the restrictions on this kind of research, put into place by his predecessor and objected to frequently by the religious right and the pro-life lobby.

28) Of the top 10 selling video games in the world, only 3 games are not made for the Wii and published by Nintendo: Activision Blizzard's *Call of Duty: Modern Warfare 2*, Ubisoft's *Assassin's Creed 2*, and the 5th installment in this survival horror series from Capcom.

29) A Boeing VC-25, a military variant of the 747, serving as a replica of this aircraft, stages a photo op around the Statue of Liberty and other locations around New York City. Residents of the city were not notified, leading to panic and evacuation of buildings in fear of another 9/11-style attack.

30) This R&B singer is arrested for assaulting his girlfriend, fellow musician Rihanna.

𝕽𝖆𝖓𝖉𝖔𝖒 𝕱𝖆𝖈𝖙, 𝕱𝖚𝖓 𝖔𝖗 𝕺𝖙𝖍𝖊𝖗𝖂𝖎𝖘𝖊

The subject of two of the questions above both have been played by Oscar winner Tom Hanks: Chesley "Sully" Sullenberger & Captain Richard Phillips.

As a side note, never travel anywhere with Tom Hanks. Look at the man's filmography:

Castaway: his plane crashed, and he was stranded on an island as the sole survivor.

Apollo 13: his spaceship exploded.

Forrest Gump: his shrimping boat was hit by a hurricane.

Greyhound: his battleship was attacked by a Nazi wolfpack, and multiple ships in his convoy were sunk.

Sully: his plane crashed.

The Terminal: his country ceased to exist while he was on board an airplane.

Joe Versus the Volcano: his boat sank and the island he was supposed to save was destroyed by a volcano.

Captain Phillips: his boat was attacked by pirates and he was taken hostage on a smaller boat.

We at the Ministry have never seen these, but we're assuming the *Polar Express* derailed after striking a polar bear; *Larry Crowne* crashed the vespa featured on the movie poster, and the *Bridge of Spies* collapsed, sending Tom Hanks into a river. (All right, we did see *Bridge of Spies*, and that does not happen. It is, however, a fantastic film, and we wholeheartedly recommend it.)

𝕬𝖓𝖘𝖂𝖊𝖗𝖘 𝖔𝖓 𝖙𝖍𝖊 𝕹𝖊𝖝𝖙 𝕻𝖆𝖌𝖊...

Answers

1) Hudson River
2) Propofol
3) *Avatar*
4) Swine Flu
5) Iron Dome
6) Spain
7) Virginia Tech
8) *The Wheel of Time*
9) Iceland
10) Photometer
11) Mahmoud Ahmadinejad
12) Chris Hemsworth
13) Sudan
14) *League of Legends*
15) Alt-right
16) Adele
17) Balloon Boy
18) Boko Haram
19) Michael Crichton
20) Greenland
21) The D.C. Sniper
22) Rick Riordan
23) *Maersk Alabama*
24) Andy Roddick
25) Sonia Sotomayor
26) George Takei
27) Embryonic stem cell research
28) *Resident Evil*
29) *Air Force One*
30) Chris Brown

Additional Facts, Fun or Otherwise, from Random Years to Properly Maintain Spacing in this Book

One of the Navy SEALs known to have participated in the rescue of Richard Phillips is Senior Chief Petty Officer Robert O'Neill, who claims to have served as the lead paratrooper on the mission. O'Neill also states he participated in the rescue of Navy SEAL Marcus Lutrell in Afghanistan, and he has said he played an instrumental role in Operation Neptune Spear, namely that he killed Osama bin Laden. This would make him a key player, not just in world events, but in Hollywood, as these stories form the basis for the movies *Captain Phillips*, *Lone Survivor*, and *Zero Dark Thirty*.

It is somewhat unusual, per the United States Navy, that the public knows this, because it is a stated part of the creed of Navy SEALs that they do not publicize or seek credit for their work. In fact, the government will not confirm or deny O'Neill's claims. There are counterclaims by other SEALs as to how much O'Neill participated in each event or who fired the fatal shots which killed bin Laden.

Despite the confusion or O'Neill's seeming interest in self-publicizing, O'Neill does have a glowing service record with two Silver Stars and four Bronze stars.

𝕴𝖓 2010...

1) An explosion on this offshore drilling rig owned by Transocean but drilling on behalf of British Petroleum leads to a fire, an oil spill, and the largest environmental disaster in American history.

2) The Melon Revolution leads to the ouster of autocrat Kurmanbek Bakiyev in this Central Asian country.

3) This landmark Supreme Court case is decided 5-4, determining that freedom of speech applies to corporations expending money toward election campaigns.

4) The eruption of Mt. Eyjafjallajökull ejects 250 million cubic meters of debris and ash into the atmosphere but manages to have a net positive environmental effect because of the disruption to this industry.

5) Following the success of *Avatar*, more films are made in this style or retrofitted to be this style, a style that has existed since 1915 and achieved initial popularity in America in the 1950s.

6) Both the current president and ex-president of this country are killed in the Smolensk Air Disaster, the crash of a Tupolev Tu-154 while making a landing approach in heavy fog

7) The Super Bowl between the New Orleans Saints and the Indianapolis Colts becomes the most watched television event in American history with an estimated 106.5 million viewers, passing the viewership for the 1983 series finale of this comedy program.

8) Alberto Giacometti's 1960 bronze sculpture *L'homme qui marche I*, literally *The Walking Man I*, sells for a record $104.3 million. It is not to be confused with a sculpture entitled *The Walking Man* by this French sculptor, best known for the sculpture *Le Penseur*.

9) A 7.0 magnitude earthquake strikes this capital of Haiti, leading to over 300,000 deaths in the deadliest earthquake recorded.

10) This Swedish author of *The Millennium Trilogy*, who passed away suddenly in 2004 before any of the trilogy were published, becomes the first author to sell 1 million e-books via Kindle.

11) This new product from Apple is announced and draws immediately snickers from female reviewers, who blame a lack of

women on the design and implementation team for a (possible) accidental menstruation reference.

12) The Kasubi Tombs, the only World Heritage Site in this country, catch fire and are almost completely destroyed.

13) This author's autobiography is officially released, one hundred years after his death as per his request, although unofficial copies have previously been published.

14) The singles "Firework" and "California Gurls" from Katy Perry are two of the five hits from this album to reach number 1 on the Billboard charts. It is the first album to have five number 1 hits since Michael Jackson's 1987 album *Bad*. A sixth single reached number 3.

15) During the European sovereign debt crisis, Standard & Poor's downgrades this country's credit rating to junk status, causing a massive stock market decline around the world and the International Monetary Fund to provide a $110 million bailout.

16) Nonviolent Chinese political dissident Liu Xiaobo becomes the third person to receive a Nobel Peace Prize while in this location, joining Aung San Suu Kyi and Carl von Ossietzky.

17) This Northern African and Middle Eastern movement begins in Tunisia and is sometimes credited to a protest by Tunisian street vendor Mohamed Bouazizi, who attempts suicide by self-immolation after confiscation of his wares and humiliation at the hands of a government official.

18) *Family Feud* picks its sixth host, this stand-up comedian, who will continue to host to this day, with over 1100 episodes under his belt.

19) Germany makes the final of these payments on a debt that goes back to 1919.

20) In response to attempts to curb data-sharing websites LimeWire and this website created by the Swedish thinktank Piratbyran, Anonymous launches cyber attacks against law firms, musicians, and copyright activists.

21) Atticus Ross and this musician, former frontman for industrial band Nine Inch Nails, compose the score for David Fincher's *The*

Social Network. They will win the Academy Award for the score in 2011.

22) The Dow Jones Industrial Average drops 9% in 36 minutes in this type of crash. It will rebound almost completely by the end of the day's trading.

23) 25 hostages, 20 of which are from Hong Kong, are taken on board a tour bus by disgruntled former police officer Rolando Mendoza, who is demanding a fair hearing regarding his termination in this Southeast Asian city. The negotiations are broadcast on television and the Internet, but collapse after ten hours, leading to a tense gun battle between police and Mendoza in which eight people are killed.

24) This country pop trio release their sophomore album *Need You Now*, which sells nearly half a million copies in its first week. In 2020, in the wake of the George Floyd protests, the band will attempt to drop 9 letters from their name, but will succeed in creating more controversy.

25) The prototype aircraft *Solar Impulse One* stays in the air for a twenty-six-hour flight, including nine hours at night, without the usage of aviation fuel. The craft is powered by this source also called a solar cell.

26) The state of Minnesota receives 17 inches of snow in a two-day period, and the accumulation on the roof of this sports stadium causes the roof to collapse.

27) Seth Grahame-Smith pens a biography of this American president (with the minor addition of some vampires, which may or may not be historically accurate.)

28) This social media platform founded by Kevin Systrom and Mike Krieger goes live. In just two years, it will be purchased by Facebook for $1 billion.

29) The team at CERN are able to create 38 stable antihydrogen atoms after capturing this for the first time.

30) At the 2010 Winter Olympics in Vancouver, the results for the men's and women's ice hockey tournament end exactly the same way, with these three teams winning gold, silver, and bronze respectively.

31) The United States Congress passes the Patient Protection and Affordable Care Act, better known as this, overcoming a Republican attempt to filibuster. Multiple lawsuits will be filed, and the Republican Congress will attempt to repeal the law 67 times in the law's first five years.

Random Fact, Fun or Otherwise

Lady Antebellum, now Lady A, have said that they originally got their name as a spur of the moment decision. After doing a photo shoot at an antebellum mansion in the south, they decided there was something cool about the word antebellum without considering what the word means. (Antebellum literally means "before the war," but in an American South context, always is in reference to the American Civil War, a timeframe and location not known as the most enlightened in America's history.)

In the wake of George Floyd's murder at the hands of the police, and the resulting outcry for racial justice, the band members decided to change the name. The public's response was not particularly receptive amid accusations of virtue signaling, not going far enough to distance themselves from the name, and attempting to draw attention away from or capitalize on the protests.

After the band's announcement, it was revealed that a Seattle-based African-American activist and blues & gospel singer by the name of Anita White had gone by the stage name of Lady A for 20 years. In an interview with *Rolling Stone*, White pointed out the tone deafness of changing one's band name in the name of racial harmony, while then usurping a name used by another African-American artist.

White asked for $10 million for the name, $5 million for herself and $5 million for charity, but Lady A took her to court to try to claim the trademark for themselves. They eventually settled out of court for an undisclosed amount.

Answers on the Next Page...

𝕬𝖓𝖘𝖜𝖊𝖗𝖘

1) *Deepwater Horizon*
2) Kyrgyzstan
3) *Citizens United v. FEC*
4) Air Travel
5) 3-D
6) Poland
7) *MASH*
8) Auguste Rodin
9) Port-au-Prince
10) Stieg Larsson
11) iPad
12) Uganda
13) Mark Twain
14) *Teenage Dream*
15) Greece
16) Prison
17) Arab Spring
18) Steve Harvey
19) War reparations (World War I reparations)
20) The Pirate Bay
21) Trent Reznor
22) Flash Crash
23) Manila
24) Lady Antebellum (Lady A)
25) Photovoltaic cell
26) Hubert H. Humphrey Metrodome
27) Abraham Lincoln
28) Instagram
29) Antimatter
30) Canada (gold); United States (Silver); Finland (Bronze)
31) Obamacare

𝕴𝖓 2011...

1) This populist movement spends 59 days encamped in Zuccotti Park, not far from the various headquarters of the organizations they are protesting.

2) With presidential support, the official government and military policy known as this is brought to an end, a giant step forward in the gay rights movement.

3) Of the top 10 highest grossest films of the year, this animation/live-action hybrid based on the works of Belgian artist Peyo is the only film that is not a sequel.

4) With aid from NATO air support, rebels in Libya are able to defeat governmental forces loyal to this man, who has ruled Libya since 1969. The rebels will kill him after taking him prisoner.

5) Due to an earthquake and a tsunami, this nuclear power plant in Japan is unable to properly cool their reactors after shutdown and radiation is released into the surrounding environment. It is the worst nuclear accident since Chernobyl.

6) This sandbox game created by Markus Persson, which will become the bestselling game of all time, is released to the general public after having a narrow release in 2009.

7) Right wing terrorist Anders Behring Breivik, claiming to be a knight defending Christian Europe, kills 12 and injures hundreds with a car bomb, and then uses a rifle and a pistol to kill 69 more at a summer camp in this country.

8) 79 commandos and a dog of this breed, commonly used by the American, Australian, and Israeli militaries, arrive in Abbottabad, Pakistan to raid the compound of Osama bin Laden.

9) H1504+65, a white dwarf star located in the Ursa Minor constellation, is measured to have the hottest temperature ever recorded at 200,000 of these degree units (approximately 360,000 Fahrenheit.)

10) Although believed by some sources to have died two years previously, this Dear Leader is officially announced as dead. In death, he will be given the title of Eternal Chairman of the Worker's Party of Korea.

11) As a part of the Arab Spring movement, protestors in Egypt began demanding the resignation of this president.

12) At the 2011 Women's World Cup, during the quarterfinal match against Brazil with the U.S. down 2-1 in extra time and down a man (woman), this midfielder sends a perfect cross to Abby Wambach who heads it home. The goal comes in the 122nd minute of the match and sends the match to penalties, which the U.S. wins 5-3.

13) Piers Morgan is tapped to replace this man's show which ran for twenty-five years on CNN. The replacement show will barely last three.

14) This IBM computer successfully defeats *Jeopardy!* champions Ken Jennings and Brad Rutter despite answering in Final Jeopardy of Game 1 that Toronto is an American city with an airport named after a World War II hero and another after a World War II battle.

15) These two actors from the film *The Fighter* sweep the Critic's Choice Awards, the Golden Globes, and the Academy Awards in the supporting actor categories. The BAFTA awards for supporting actors will go to Geoffrey Rush and Helena Bonham Carter for *The King's Speech*.

16) The final space shuttle mission comes to an end with this shuttle touching down in Florida. It will remain in Florida as a museum piece for the Kennedy Space Center Visitor Center.

17) The islands of Samoa and Tokelau are moved from the western side to the eastern side of this artificial barrier in order to better accommodate the time zones of their main trading partners.

18) At a supermarket in Tucson, this Congresswoman is shot in the head along with several others by a paranoid, right-wing schizophrenic. She will recover, and her future husband will become a senator from Arizona.

19) The United States changes its military doctrine so that this kind of attack is considered casus belli.

20) The Rugby World Cup Final between these two teams is the lowest scoring final in the history of the tournament, 8-7.

21) This acapella group wins the third season of *The Sing-Off* and finds a massive following on YouTube. Their first two albums of

covers and Christmas songs will be released to solid reviews and will sell over 500,000 copies combined.

22) British Culture Secretary Jeremy Hunt claims that 2 billion people watched this event, although this number is debated. The event did set a record with 72 million people watching the live stream on YouTube.

23) This video game and entertainment service goes dark for 23 days after hackers break into the service and compromise the data of over 77 million users.

24) Popular protests against the Ba'athist government in this country will lead to a multifactional civil war between the government, foreign powers, terrorist organizations, independence movements, and various militias.

25) In response to vocal conspiracy theories coming from the right, including from a future President of the United States, President Obama releases this long form document.

26) Apple CEO Steve Jobs passes away from complications due to pancreatic cancer, after foregoing standard treatment in favor of this type of treatment, characterized by unproven methods and spiritualism.

27) Protestors in this country storm the embassy of the United Kingdom, leading to a diplomatic crisis and the U.K. recalling their representatives while expelling those of the offending country.

28) This American college student is freed after being acquitted on retrial in Italy, following her 2007 conviction in the murder of her roommate, fellow exchange student Meredith Kercher.

29) After having over $500 million in loans approved by the Obama administration, this solar panel company files for bankruptcy and becomes a talking point for Republican legislators regarding government waste.

30) The Dallas Mavericks, owned by this billionaire entrepreneur, win the NBA title.

Random Fact, Fun or Otherwise

Within the cult of personality which went along with Kim Jong Il, we have been treated to many "facts" about the North Korean leader over the years, including:

- A double rainbow appeared over the spot of his birth along with a new star in the night sky.
- He learned to walk at three weeks and talk at eight weeks.
- Over a three year period in college, he wrote 1500 books and six operas.
- During his first time playing golf, he shot a -38, including 11 holes in one.
- His hair style and jumpsuits made him a global fashion icon, imitated across the world.
- He never had to use the bathroom.

Answers on the Next Page...

Answers

1) Occupy Wall Street
2) Don't Ask; Don't Tell
3) *The Smurfs*
4) Muammar Gaddafi
5) Fukushima Nuclear Plant
6) *Minecraft*
7) Norway
8) Belgian Malinois
9) Kelvin
10) Kim Jong Il
11) Hosni Mubarak
12) Megan Rapinoe
13) Larry King
14) Watson
15) Christian Bale & Melissa Leo
16) *Atlantis*
17) International Dateline
18) Gabby Giffords
19) Cyber attack
20) New Zealand & France
21) Pentatonix
22) The Wedding of Prince William & Catherine Middleton
23) Sony PlayStation Network
24) Syria
25) His birth certificate
26) Alternative medicine
27) Iran
28) Amanda Knox
29) Solyndra
30) Mark Cuban

Additional Facts, Fun or Otherwise, from Random Years to Properly Maintain Spacing in this Book

In 2010, one of the new words introduced was the term libfix. Most people use libfixes every day, but are not even aware of what they are. Libfix was coined by Arnold Zwicky, a linguistics professor from Stanford, taking the prefix from "liberated" and the suffix from "affix."

A libfix is a back-formation when prefixes or suffixes associated with one word are used to create a new meaning and then appended to other words to create a subsequent word. (We at the Ministry of Trivia know that previous sentence was basically gobbledygook, but an example will provide the necessary clarity.)

An example would be the word marathon, which has had the -athon used in words such as telethon, walkathon, and hackathon. Athon has no etymological meaning in and of itself.

Using the suffix -gate to any type of scandal is a further example. A good example of a prefix is the use of franken- to describe any example of humanity messing with nature: Frankenfood, Frankenplant, etc.

In 2012...

1) On this calendar date, the last day of the 13th b'ak'tan of the Mayan Calendar, the world surprisingly does not end despite the belief of new age mystics and Roland Emmerich.

2) Norwegian crime comedy-drama *Lilyhammer* becomes the first exclusive content offered by this provider.

3) This weather event strikes and does extensive damage to New York, New Jersey, and New England just before the American presidential election. Some pundits will describe the event as a positive for Obama's reelection hopes, as his visits to the affected areas gives him an opportunity to look "presidential."

4) Scientists at CERN end a 40-year search for this predicted particle, sometimes called the "God particle."

5) This film series reaches its 50th anniversary and releases the 23rd in the series, the last to feature Judi Dench.

6) This Scotsman playing for the Great Britain tennis team at the London Olympics wins the gold medal against Roger Federer in a match staged at Wimbledon. It is the first male Brit to win at Wimbledon since 1936 although it does not count as "winning at Wimbledon." He will however win at Wimbledon in 2013.

7) Militias from the northern area of this African nation proclaim a new nation for the Tuareg people named Azawad. They will quickly lose control of the revolution as Islamist and Al-Qaeda-affiliated organizations will take control, while the central government appeals to outside powers for assistance.

8) The release of the film *Innocence of Muslims* leads to worldwide protests from the Muslim community, violence, and is initially believed to be responsible for an attack on the U.S. consulate in this Libyan city.

9) NASA Flight Director Bobak Ferdowsi becomes a temporary Internet celebrity when his mohawk hair style is featured prominently in the video shown of the NASA control room during the landing of this rover on Mars.

10) Sometimes called a one hit wonder, this Australian musician has a massive hit with "Someone that I Used to Know," which will become one of the bestselling digital singles of all time

11) Captain Francesco Schettino of the cruise ship *Costa Concordia* runs the ship into a rock formation, and when it starts to list, commits this cardinal sin in maritime tradition. He will receive a 15-year sentence for manslaughter related to those who died in the accident with an additional year for violating the maritime tradition.

12) Publishers announce that this 32-volume work, published and updated since 1768 in the United Kingdom, will no longer be printed in book form.

13) While watching a screening of *The Dark Knight Rises* in this American city, 12 people are murdered and 70 more are injured by James Holmes.

14) The Gurlitt Collection, a trove of art missing since World War II is found in Munich. It is believed to have been collected by Hildebrand Gurlitt, one of the four authorized art dealers for this man, an artist in his own right.

15) This song by South Korean musician Psy becomes a worldwide sensation and introduces K-Pop to much of the world.

16) As part of the Red Bull Statos project, this man becomes the first human to break the sound barrier unassisted by propellant. After travelling 24 miles into the air by helium balloon, he skydives, eventually reaching Mach 1.25.

17) For the first time in 852 weeks, this morning show broadcast on ABC captures more viewers than NBC's *Today*.

18) This second year Denver Broncos quarterback is traded to the New York Jets, despite having a 7-4 record and winning a playoff game the year before. The impetus for the trade is the Broncos signing free agent quarterback Peyton Manning.

19) Cannabis is legalized for recreational use in this American state, the first state to allow it for non-medical purposes.

20) The release of *The Hobbit: An Unexpected Journey* marks a first for high frame rate film. It was shot at 48 frames per second, rather than this industry standard.

21) After 17 people are killed in a dispute between migrant farmers and the police trying to evict them, President Fernando Lugo of this country is impeached and removed from office. Many of his

supporters as well as leaders in neighboring countries view this as a manufactured crisis and a back-door coup d'état.

22) A novel coronavirus first identified in a man in Jeddah leads to an outbreak in Western Asia of the virus that bares this name, named after the location where it began.

23) This Rochester, New York-based company founded in 1892, formerly included in the thirty blue chip companies which comprise the Dow Jones Industrial Average, and victim of the digital revolution, files for bankruptcy protection.

24) At the iHeartRadio Music Festival, this frontman for Green Day stops playing "Basket Case," goes on an expletive-laden rant, destroys a guitar, and flips off the concert organizers. He will check into rehab a few days later.

25) One year after this winningest college football coach of all time is fired from his head coaching position at Penn State University, he dies, following a battle with cancer. His legacy is tarnished by the conclusions drawn by former FBI director Louis Freeh, which state he helped cover up the sexual abuse perpetrated by his defensive coordinator Jerry Sandusky.

26) Dartmouth College researchers identify that organic foods which contain organic brown rice syrup as a substitute for this much maligned sweetener have a higher concentration of arsenic due to rice husk's ability to absorb higher amounts of environmental arsenic.

27) Lonesome George, the last of these animals from the Pinta Island subspecies, dies at the age of 102. He had spent 41 years as the last member of his subspecies.

28) After shooting 17-year-old Travyon Martin, George Zimmerman is initially not prosecuted by Florida district attorneys, who cite this law, which runs counter to other states' duty-to-retreat self-defense laws. Eventually succumbing to public pressure, prosecutors will bring a case, but Zimmerman will be found not guilty.

29) After five years, Turkish-American adventurer Erden Eruc becomes the first person to complete a solo circumnavigation of the Earth, using only this means.

30) This bakery-based food company announces that it will file for bankruptcy and liquidate its assets, sending shoppers to stores searching for Twinkies. (Little to no concern is shown for the potential permanent loss of the public's access to Snowballs.) The company will be brough back by new owners in 2013, Twinkies (and Snowballs) included.

Random Fact, Fun or Otherwise

The Gurlitt Collection was initially announced as a "Nazi loot discovery," and wild estimates were reported that the horde was worth in excess of a billion dollars, which was extreme for the approximately 1500 pieces of art which were included.

The art was discovered as part of an investigation by German authorities into collector Cornelius Gurlitt on suspicion of tax evasion. The authorities seized the collection, but Gurlitt requested it be returned on the grounds he had committed no crime himself. However, he agreed that the authorities could hold the pieces while they verified there were no looted pieces in the collection. In 2014, the collection was returned to Gurlitt, but he died shortly thereafter and left the entire collection to a museum in Switzerland, which accepted the collection except for any pieces that might have been looted.

1039 pieces of art were reviewed with 315 being identified as confiscated from German museums as "deviant art," 28 identified as pre-war pieces not having not been looted, and 42 were not reviewed due to being post-war, mass produced, or associated with a museum. A handful have been returned to their rightful owners, and provenance investigations continue on the remaining.

The collection included works from Monet, Renoir, Cezanne, Gaugin, Matisse, Degas, Delacroix, Toulouse-Lautrec, Chagall, Manet, Rodin, Munch, and Kandinsky.

Although no official valuation has ever been released, at least two pieces have sold for $10-$20 million, and there are multiple million dollar pieces in the collection.

Answers on the Next Page...

Answers

1) December 21
2) Netflix
3) Superstorm Sandy (Hurricane Sandy)
4) Higgs boson
5) James Bond Series
6) Andy Murray
7) Mali
8) Benghazi
9) *Curiosity*
10) Gotye
11) Not going down with the ship (evacuating before all other souls aboard are saved)
12) *Encyclopedia Brittanica*
13) Aurora
14) Adolph Hitler
15) *Gangnam Style*
16) Felix Baumgartner
17) *Good Morning America*
18) Tim Tebow
19) Washington
20) 24 Frames per second
21) Peru
22) Middle Eastern Respiratory Syndrome (MERS)
23) Kodak
24) Billy Joe Armstrong
25) Joe Paterno
26) High-fructose corn syrup
27) Tortoise
28) Stand-your-ground law
29) Human-powered transportation (canoes, bikes, and legs)
30) Hostess

𝕴𝖓 2013...

1) This man quits his job, the first to quit the position since 1415, and the first to do so voluntarily since 1294.

2) While working for this military and intelligence contractor, Edward Snowden releases a trove of classified documents, many related to the PRISM data mining program and then flees to Russia.

3) This Disney film, the highest grossing film of the year, leads to a. increase in children named Elsa in both the U.S. and U.K.

4) In a battle between these two head coaching brothers, the Baltimore Ravens defeat the San Francisco 49ers 34-31 in Super Bowl XLVII.

5) After being "bumped" from every episode of *Jimmy Kimmel Live*, this actor stages his revenge and takes over the show.

6) *Self-portrait Wearing a White-feathered Bonnet*, believed to be a painting by this master until rejected by an art historian in 1968, is announced to have been reattributed to said master.

7) July 4 television broadcasting in the United States does not include a nationwide broadcast of this American orchestra for the first time since 1987.

8) The collapse of Rana Plaza in Bangladesh kills 1100 workers, mostly workers in this industry, triggering protests and greater government involvement in building standards. The building owner and many others will be charged with murder due to their knowledge that the building was unsafe and still requiring workers to occupy the building.

9) This American city is almost completely shut down as a manhunt carries on for two bombers who have killed 3 people with explosives and murdered one campus police officer.

10) This early grunge band fires lead singer Scott Weiland and brings in Chester Bennington from Linkin Park.

11) In Nairobi, Kenya, the Westgate Shopping Mall is attacked by members of this East African Al-Qaeda affiliate, who massacre over 60 civilians.

12) This video game from Naughty Dog sells 1.3 million copies in its first week, receives rave reviews, and in retrospect, will be

considered one of the greatest games of all time. It will later be adapted into a series starring Pedro Pascal by HBO.

13) Somewhat oddly, this Washington, D.C.-based hockey blog, named after a quote attributed to Russian-born winger Alex Ovechkin, is the first English-speaking news source to break the story of the Chelyabinsk Meteor. It is believed to be the largest atmospheric meteor burst since Tunguska.

14) At the MTV music awards, Miley Cyrus sparks controversy by performing this dance with Robin Thicke.

15) After serving as interim president after the death of Hugo Chavez, this man wins the Venezuelan presidential election by a relatively narrow margin of 200,000 votes.

16) In the landmark supreme court case *United States v. Windsor*, the Supreme Court determines that the federal government must recognize same sex marriage for couples married in a state where same sex marriage is legal. The ruling guts this 1996 bill signed into law by Bill Clinton.

17) The Joint Plan of Action to curb Iran's nuclear program in exchange for an easing of sanctions is agreed to between Iran and the P5+1 countries, which are the five permanent members of the UN Security Council and this country.

18) The tennis doubles championships for all four majors as well as the Olympic gold medal are held by one pair, these American twins.

19) This Canadian short story writer, author of the critically acclaimed collections *Who Do You Think You Are?* and *The Love of a Good Woman*, receives the Nobel Prize for literature.

20) The combined expiration of the 2010 Tax Relief Act and required, scheduled spending cuts under the Budget Control Act of 2011 become known as this two-word phrase. The issues and the possible recession they would have caused are thwarted by the passage of the American Taxpayer Relief Act.

21) Because of the deployment of these stealth aircraft by the American government during maneuvers with the South Korean military, North Korean president Kim-Jong Un orders his

generals to develop strike packages for rocket strikes on the U.S. mainland. China is forced to step in to cool down tensions.

22) Software organization Defense Distributed releases schematics for making "wiki weapons" with these devices. The Department of State sends them a cease and desist request due to accused violations of The International Traffic in Arms Regulations.

23) This film with only two live action roles and five voice rolls ends its run as the highest grossing film for its two main stars, Sandra Bullock and George Clooney.

24) This former presidential candidate is selected as Hilary Clinton's replacement as secretary of state by Barack Obama. He will later be selected as Joe Biden's special envoy on climate.

25) In a 5-4 decision in *Shelby County v Holder*, the Supreme Court guts this 1965 law.

26) This robotics company spun off of the Massachusetts Institute of Technology in 1992 and famous for its BigDog robot is acquired by Google.

27) John Charles Beale is convicted of felony theft while working for the EPA after getting paid for days he took off without using vacation time while supposedly working for this clandestine organization. Later, he will confess that he spent those days at his home, reading and exercising.

28) This British street artist spends a month-long residency in New York City, revealing a new piece of art graffitied every day.

29) This University of Notre Dame linebacker does not play well in a 42-14 defeat to Alabama in the college football national title game. It later emerges that his alleged girlfriend, who supposedly died of cancer, did not exist, and that he was the victim of catfishing.

30) This ridiculously over-the-top, brainless horror-comedy starring Ian Ziering and Tara Reid makes its debut on the SyFy Channel. It will become an almost instant cult classic that spawns five sequels and several spinoffs.

𝕽𝖆𝖓𝖉𝖔𝖒 𝕱𝖆𝖈𝖙, 𝕱𝖚𝖓 𝖔𝖗 𝕺𝖙𝖍𝖊𝖗𝖜𝖎𝖘𝖊

The case of Manti Te'o was at least partially responsible for mainstreaming the idea of catfishing in the American consciousness, although the term began with the 2010 documentary *Catfish*.

In 2012, in the midst of his senior season and a Heisman Trophy campaign, Te'o announced that his girlfriend Lennay Kekua had lost her battle with cancer, a form of leukemia that was diagnosed after a car accident. The media made a big deal about the seemingly legitimate human-interest story, and Te'o continued to play, stating he promised Lennay that he would.

After receiving an anonymous tip in early 2013, *Deadspin* reporters Timothy Burke and Jack Dickey published an article alleging that Kekua did not exist, and that Ronaiah "Naya" Tuiasosopo had perpetrated this hoax.

Tuiasosopo, who had meant Te'o once and claimed to have fallen in love with him, created the Lennay character as an effort to get to know Te'o better and pursue a relationship with him. Te'o eventually admitted that he had lied to his parents and others about meeting Lennay in person, because he did not think anyone would understand how he could be in a serious relationship with someone he only knew online and over the phone.

𝕬𝖓𝖘𝖜𝖊𝖗𝖘 𝖔𝖓 𝖙𝖍𝖊 𝕹𝖊𝖝𝖙 𝕻𝖆𝖌𝖊...

Answers

1) Pope Benedict XVI (The Pope)
2) Booz Allen Hamilton
3) *Frozen*
4) Jim Harbaugh & John Harbaugh
5) Matt Damon
6) Rembrandt
7) Boston Pops
8) Garment industry
9) Boston
10) Stone Temple Pilots
11) Al-Shabaab
12) *The Last of Us*
13) *Russian Machine Never Breaks*
14) Twerking
15) Nicolas Maduro
16) Defense of Marriage Act
17) Germany
18) The Bryan Brothers
19) Alice Munro
20) Fiscal Cliff
21) B-2 Bombers
22) 3-D Printer
23) *Gravity*
24) John Kerry
25) The Voting Rights Act
26) Boston Dynamics
27) CIA
28) Banksy
29) Manti Te'o
30) *Sharknado*

Additional Facts, Fun or Otherwise, from Random Years to Properly Maintain Spacing in this Book

If I were to tell you that one pair of American siblings dominated tennis in the early 2000s and 2010s, you would be forgiven if you assumed that I was talking about Venus & Serena Williams. Not that you shouldn't be thinking of them as dominant, they absolutely are, but one pair of siblings does tend to fly under the radar and that is the Bryan Brothers.

Bob and Mike Bryan are twins (specifically mirror twins- one is right-handed and the other left-handed, giving them better court coverage), who won 16 major championships playing together as doubles partners. They made 30 majors finals, so also have 14 runners-up trophies for majors.

Mike has two additional major titles from partnering with Jack Sock while Bob was recovering from surgery, and has 4 major championships and 2 runners-up from playing mixed doubles, partnering with Lisa Raymond, Liezel Huber, Katarina Srebotnik, and Bethanie Matteck-Sands. One of his victories and one of his defeats in a mixed doubles final was against his brother Bob.

Bob has 7 mixed doubles titles out of 9 appearances, partnering with Venus Williams, Martina Navratilova, Victoria Azarenka, Liezel Huber, Katarina Srebotnik, Vera Zvonareva, and Samantha Stosur.

The brothers won the 2007 Davis Cup, the 2012 Olympic gold in doubles tennis, and from 2012-2013 completed a non-calendar year Golden Slam- winning all 4 majors and an Olympic gold medal. They held the world no. 1 doubles ranking for 438 weeks, and a record 139 consecutive weeks.

In 2014…

1) The Russian military and Russian-leaning separatists seize critical areas of this peninsula, leading to annexation and international condemnation.

2) This host country is crushed in the semifinals of the 2014 FIFA World Cup 7-1 by eventual champions Germany. They will also lose the 3rd place match to the Netherlands.

3) This second highest grossing film of the year is adapted from approximately 50 pages of its source material. The namesake event for the film lasts less than half a chapter, at least partially because the narrator is unconscious for much of it.

4) An outbreak of this hemorrhagic fever in West Africa peaks and triggers panic in the United States despite the number of cases being limited to four.

5) After crushing the Iraqi army, this insurgent and terrorist group proclaims a new caliphate, leading to the U.S. and other countries to order air strikes against the organization

6) This American soprano becomes the first opera singer to perform the national anthem at the Super Bowl.

7) The third entry in this video game series, subtitled *Inquisition*, is released and immediately seen as an upgrade from the second game. A cinematic cut scene where characters come together after a defeat to sing a hymn entitled, "The Dawn Will Come," is lauded as one of the best scenes and best musical moments in video game history.

8) The abduction of nearly 300 teenagers from The Government Girls Secondary School in Chibok, Nigeria leads to worldwide outrage and the trending social media movement known by this hashtag.

9) The FCC votes unanimously to eliminate this rule which prohibits the broadcasting of local NFL games that have not sold out.

10) A military junta is established in this southeast Asian nation following a coup d'état, the 12th coup since 1932.

11) Historian Hildegard Hammerschmidt-Hummel announces that she has determined conclusively that two portraits are in fact of this man, who died 397 years before.

12) This First Minister of Scotland and leader of the Scottish National Party resigns both positions after the referendum on Scottish independence fails with 55% of Scots voting to remain in the U.K.

13) Two different flights from Malaysian Airlines experience tragedy with Flight 17 being shot down by the Russian Air Force and this flight vanishing without a trace over the Indian Ocean.

14) This San Francisco Giant pitcher wins Games 1 and 5 in the World Series (including a complete game shutout in game 5) and pitches 5 innings in relief to earn a save in the deciding game 7. He is voted the MVP of the series.

15) Belgium becomes the first country to legalize this for terminally ill patients of any age

16) *Blood Swept Lands and Seas of Red* premiers in London. Consisting of nearly 900,000 ceramic red poppies, the installation marks the centenary of this event

17) At the Winter Olympics in Sochi, this United States pairing captures the nation's attention and wins America's first gold medal in ice dancing.

18) At the Academy Awards, this actor introduces Idina Menzel as Adele Nazeem during the lead up to Menzel singing "Let it Go."

19) A member of the Bharatiya Janata Party, this man leads his party to a parliamentary majority and becomes prime minister of India.

20) Taylor Swift releases this album, which sells almost 1.3 million copies in the first week. By 2023, it will sell nearly 13 million copies and will be rereleased as "Taylor's Version."

21) The shooting of unarmed African-American Michael Brown triggers protests and riots in this city, part of the greater St. Louis area.

22) Houthi forces seize this capital of Yemen, triggering a Yemeni civil war.

23) The Obama administration announces that the review of this controversial oil pipeline running from Canada to Nebraska will continue indefinitely.

24) The 200th episode of this television show is told not from the point of view of main character Ted Mosby, but from that of his future wife.

25) After 54 years of hostility, President Obama briefly normalizes relations with this country. In 2016, he will become the first president since Calvin Coolidge to visit it.

26) In order to save money in this American city, the city government stops purchasing its drinking water from Lake Huron and chooses instead to attempt to purify water from the local river. 100,000 residents will be exposed to high lead levels because of the switch, and it is also a possible cause for an outbreak of Legionnaire's Disease.

27) The planned release of this comedy film starring James Franco, Seth Rogen, and Randall Park causes uproar in North Korea and possibly leads to a cyber attack on film studio Sony Pictures, who are responsible for the film's distribution.

28) A massive cold wave strikes the United States, creating an abnormally frigid winter in the northeastern, midwestern, and mid-Atlantic areas, is credited with adding this two word phrase to America's weather lexicon.

29) Three million people stream a debate entitled "Is Creation a Viable Method of Origins?" between this Creationist and Young Earther, who will later build a replica of Noah's Ark as a tourist trap, and this TV host and self-proclaimed "Science Guy."

30) After revelations that he had made racist remarks surface, this owner of the Los Angeles Clippers is fined $2.5 million by the NBA and given a lifetime ban from basketball.

𝕽𝖆𝖓𝖉𝖔𝖒 𝕱𝖆𝖈𝖙, 𝕱𝖚𝖓 𝖔𝖗 𝕺𝖙𝖍𝖊𝖗𝖜𝖎𝖘𝖊

The debate between creationist Ken Ham and Bill Nye might be viewed as a debate victory for Nye, yet a moral victory for Ham. Discussions with scientists have revealed that they tend to side with Nye, despite Nye not being an evolutionary biologist by training and stating that this was not his field during the debate. Even a few evangelicals conceded that Nye won (or that Ham lost for not bringing up more of what they considered inconsistencies with science).

In the debate itself, Ham brought up the idea that there is a difference between historical science and observable science; essentially, that science may not be immutable, and since modern day scientists were not present in the past, they cannot definitively say that scientific laws operated differently in the past than they do now. Nye's response was to question why we should question that natural laws have changed over time. Nye consistently brought evidence to his arguments, on the other hand, while Ham generally referred to the Bible as his evidence.

When asked what would change their minds, Nye stated he would be swayed by new evidence; Ham responded, "Nothing."

Many think that Ham's victory came in the form of giving the Creationist and Intelligent Design movement an undeserved legitimacy. Ham also credited it with helping him raised the money for his Ark Encounter, a replica of Noah's Ark, which was once damaged by heavy rains.

𝕬𝖓𝖘𝖜𝖊𝖗𝖘 𝖔𝖓 𝖙𝖍𝖊 𝕹𝖊𝖝𝖙 𝕻𝖆𝖌𝖊...

Answers

1) Crimea
2) Brazil
3) *The Hobbit: The Battle of the Five Armies*
4) Ebola
5) ISIS (ISIL or Islamic State of Iraq and the Levant)
6) Renee Fleming
7) *Dragon Age*
8) #BringBackOurGirls
9) Blackout rule
10) Thailand
11) William Shakespeare
12) Alex Salmond
13) Malaysian Airlines Flight 370
14) Madison Bumgarner
15) Euthanasia
16) World War I
17) Meryl Davis & Charlie White
18) John Travolta
19) Narendra Modi
20) *1989*
21) Ferguson
22) Sanaa
23) Keystone XL Pipeline
24) *How I Met Your Mother*
25) Cuba
26) Flint
27) *The Interview*
28) Polar Vortex
29) Bill Nye & Ken Ham
30) Donald Sterling

Additional Facts, Fun or Otherwise, from Random Years to Properly Maintain Spacing in this Book

For a fraudster and someone milking the government, John Charles Beale certainly had some strange schemes, some of them bordering on unnecessary. During his work with the EPA, because of his heavy travel schedule due to EPA business, rumors began to abound that he was a secret agent, working for the CIA. What was he to do with that rumor other than claim it was true and start taking advantage of it? He began entering D.O. on various days on his calendar, short for Directorate of Operations, the covert branch of the CIA. Generally, when he was theoretically checking in with his CIA handlers, he treated those days as a free day off.

In 2002, he started receiving a subsidized parking space because of the malaria he had acquired in Vietnam, a disease he did not have from a place he had never been. For three years, he claimed to be working on an EPA project in California and asked for nearly $60,000 in travel reimbursement, when he was actually just visiting family.

When he retired in 2011, he continued to draw his salary and bonus, and when asked about it, stated he was still working for the CIA even though he was retired from his "real job."

The lies stopped working in 2013. Beale spent 32 months in jail, but to this day, some of his co-workers believe he was actually a CIA agent, and that he was "taking one for the team" when he got caught.

In 2015...

1) Two al-Qaeda terrorists assault a French satirical periodical's office, killing twelve and injuring more in response to cartoons depicting the prophet Muhammad. Amidst a worldwide outpouring of grief and sympathy, this three-word French phrase becomes a popular means to demonstrate solidarity.

2) *Dawn*, a NASA probe sent to this celestial body, becomes the first probe to visit a dwarf planet.

3) This sequel/reboot, the fifth film in the science-fiction franchise, becomes the first American film to gross $400 million in ticket sales while failing to break the $100 million barrier in the United States. The only previous film to achieve this feat was the French film *Intouchables*.

4) The World Health Organization declares that this disease, also known as German measles, has been eradicated from the Americas.

5) In the U.K. parliamentary elections, this political party, generally considered the third largest in the United Kingdom, is absolutely clobbered at the polls, going from 57 seats to only eight.

6) The main cast of this 1980s American television show reunites, without Dustin Diamond or Lark Voorhies, for a sketch on *The Tonight Show*.

7) This controversial sports figure resigns his position after the FBI announces they are investigating corruption allegations against the sporting body he leads.

8) This foreign leader gives a speech before the United States Congress urging them not to support the Nuclear Deal being negotiated by the Obama administration, the UN Security Council, Germany, and Iran.

9) This rock band sets a record for longest span of time in between number 1 singles in the Billboard Mainstream Rock charts as "Coming for You" hits number 1. In 1997, "Gone Away" went to number 1.

10) A bout between these two welterweight boxers, in the works since 2009, finally goes through, to rather disappointing reviews. The 12 round fight goes to unanimous decision after a highly

defensive affair. Although dubbed "The Fight of the Century" in the lead-up, some critics will later attribute the title, "Better Never than Late" to the bout.

11) Rachel Dolezal is forced to resign as a chapter president of this organization, is fired from her post as Africana Studies chair at Eastern Washington University, and is removed from her position as chair of the Spokane Police Ombudsman Commission after it is revealed that she has been masquerading as African-American, despite being white.

12) With 20 seconds remaining in Super Bowl XLIX and 1 yard away from a touchdown to take the lead, the Seattle Seahawks opt not to hand the ball to star running back Marshawn Lynch, instead calling a pass. The result is Russell Wilson throwing an interception to this New England Patriots cornerback.

13) Queen Elizabeth II officially becomes the longest reigning British sovereign, surpassing this woman, her great-great-grandmother.

14) As part of a performance art piece, Columbia University student Emma Sulkowicz carries this fifty-pound item around campus and to her graduation ceremony, stating the performance will end when her accused rapist is expelled or leaves the university. Although lauded by some art critics and especially by victims' rights' advocates, the piece does not achieve its goal as Sulkowicz's alleged attacker is not expelled and files a lawsuit against Columbia for allowing the project to continue.

15) At the 2015 FIFA Woman's World Cup final, the United States scores four goals in the first 16 minutes, three of them by this forward, and cruises to a 5-2 victory over Japan.

16) *The Witcher 3: The Wild Hunt*, based on the fantasy novels of this author, is launched with Polish President Bronislaw Komorowski and Prime Minister Ewa Kopacz visiting publisher CD Projekt Red to help celebrate.

17) This American newsman, anchor for *NBC Nightly News*, apologizes for stating he was in a helicopter that was shot down in Iraq in 2003. He will be suspended for six months and eventually will lose his anchor position, but will be reassigned to the breaking news desk at MSNBC.

18) The first observation of these cosmic waves, long inferred to exist and validating aspects of the theory of general relativity, occurs simultaneously by LIGO and Virgo Installations. The findings will not be announced until the next year

19) This former Olympic gold medal winning decathlete and reality show star appears on the cover of *Vanity Fair* magazine, requesting to be called by a new name.

20) After winning his first major championship at Augusta in April, this American golfer wins the next major as well, the 2015 U.S. Open at Chambers Bay. Lauded as a potential successor to Tiger Woods, he will go on to only win 1 more major in the next eight years.

21) After successfully relaunching *Star Trek* in 2009, this director helms the relaunch of another franchise with this film, the highest grossing film of the year and the third film to eclipse $2 billion in ticket sales.

22) In response to the racially motivated attack at a black church in Charleston, activist Bree Newsome is arrested after climbing a flag pole and removing this emblem.

23) Despite the 5-4 Supreme Court decision in *Obergefell v. Hodges* establishing the legality of same-sex marriage in the United States, this county clerk in Kentucky achieves her fifteen minutes of notoriety for refusing to perform the duty of issuing marriage licenses to same sex couples.

24) After years of hyping their climate friendly vehicles, this auto manufacturer is charged with deliberately deceiving emissions tests, using software to show emissions as 40 times less under test circumstances.

25) This horse wins the Triple Crown, the first to do so since Affirmed in 1978.

26) Tensions escalate between NATO and Russia as this NATO member nation shoots down a Russian fighter which has violated its air space.

27) British pop group/boy band One Direction goes from a fivesome to a foursome with the departure of this singer.

28) This American store, which began as a store for ham operators before expanding into hobbyist electronics and telecom, is delisted from the New York Stock Exchange and files for Chapter 11 bankruptcy protection.

29) SpaceX successfully recovers one of these reusable rockets after a launch for the first time. Recoverable rockets are an essential aspect of SpaceX's plan to make space colonization and exploration less expensive.

30) The album *Morning Phase* by this musician wins Album of the Year at the Grammys, prompting Kanye West to once again leap on stage, although allegedly in jest this time. (He did say later that he believed Beyoncé should have won this year too.)

Random Fact, Fun or Otherwise

The feud between Kanye West & Taylor Swift feels like a kind of rivalry destined be one of those great, titanic battles of history or mythology, born of enmity, quenched only in blood, like York & Lancaster, Montagues & Capulets, or Marius & Sulla. Indeed, we at the Ministry suspect that in the decades to come, long after the deaths of Kanye and Taylor (surely at the hands of each other), the epic tale will inspire a multi-season, generation-spanning Netflix extravaganza, or at the very least, a Klingon opera.

The feud began at the MTV Video Music Awards (Children, MTV used to show music videos before YouTube was thing). After Swift won Best Female Video for "You Belong with Me," Kanye climbed onstage, interrupted Swift's speech, took the microphone from her, and proclaimed in so many words that Beyoncé should have won. Swift left the stage without finishing her speech. (Beyoncé, to her credit, invited Swift back onto the stage when she won an award later in the show.)

Kanye's actions were derided across numerous circles, and he initially apologized, but then recanted said apology. The years dragged on, and the feud appeared to be ended, as the two had patched up their relationship with the help of Jay-Z, a mutual friend to both of them.

Then Kanye released "Famous." The song features the line, "I feel like me and Taylor might still have sex / Why? I made that bitch famous," and the music video features a naked wax doll of Swift. Kanye claimed that he had spoken to Swift and secured her permission for the lyrics, a claim she denied.

After a speech from Swift appeared to shade West at the 2016 Grammy Awards, Kim Kardashian-West, Kanye's wife, released an edited version of the phone call between Swift and Kanye where they discussed the lyrics. The video appeared to provide vindication for Kanye and caused some of the public and the media to turn on Swift.

In 2020, the full, unedited clip was released, once again proving that Swift's recollections of the conversation were correct, and that Kanye had not informed Swift about the full extent of the lyrics or the naked doll.

The backlash Swift received in 2016 caused her to step away from music for a year, but after the truth became known in 2020, she returned to being pop music's largest superstar. Kanye, meanwhile, ran unsuccessfully for president in 2020; at times supported both Barack Obama and Donald Trump; publicly bullied Pete Davidson over Davidson's relationship with his ex-wife; and lost most of his sponsorships for a series of antisemitic statements.

Answers on the Next Page...

𝔄𝔫𝔰𝔴𝔢𝔯𝔰

1) Je Suis Charlie
2) Ceres
3) *Terminator: Genisys*
4) Rubella
5) Liberal Democrats
6) *Saved by the Bell*
7) Sepp Blatter
8) Benjamin Netanyahu
9) Offspring
10) Floyd Mayweather & Manny Pacquiao
11) NAACP
12) Malcolm Butler
13) Queen Victoria
14) A mattress
15) Carli Lloyd
16) Andrzej Sapkowski
17) Brian Williams
18) Gravitational waves
19) Caitlyn Jenner (previously Bruce Jenner)
20) Jordan Spieth
21) J.J. Abrams
22) Confederate flag (technically, the battle flag of the Confederate Army of Northern Virginia or the Confederate Navy Jack)
23) Kim Davis
24) Volkswagen
25) American Pharoah
26) Turkey
27) Zayn Malik
28) Radio Shack
29) Falcon 9
30) Beck

𝕴𝖓 2016...

1) Joaquin Guzman, better known by this nickname, is arrested after his second escape from prison. The leader of the Sinaloa Cartel is considered to be one of the most powerful drug traffickers in the world at the time of his arrest.

2) Sheikh Nimr, a member of this sect of Islam, is executed by the Saudi Arabian government for leading protests against discrimination against his sect and for calling for free elections.

3) At the Super Bowl 50 halftime show, Beyonce draws both praise and criticism for her outfit inspired by the Black Panthers and performs "Formation," the first released song from this album, her sixth.

4) The World Health Organization declares this virus transmitted by mosquitos, which carries the possibilities of developing birth defects, such as microcephaly, in pregnancies, and Guillain-Barre Syndrome in adults, to have reached epidemic status. By the end of the epidemic, which originated in Brazil, it is estimated that 1.5 million people are infected.

5) The Islamic State carries off two suicide bombings in this country, one at Brussels Airport and one at Maelbeek metro station.

6) This augmented reality mobile game is released by Niantic. By 2018, it will have 147 million active users and will make $6 billion, despite using a freemium model.

7) The leak of a collection of documents, collectively dubbed this, are published by *Suddeutsche Zeitung* after being acquired from law firm Mossack Fonseca, revealing the shell companies the rich and powerful use to shield money from tax responsibilities.

8) Having previously served as the mayor of Davao City, this Filipino populist runs for president and wins. His caustic, aggressive style is compared to U.S. President Donald Trump, and he immediately ratchets up the War on Drugs, leading to between 5,000 and 20,000 extrajudicial killings.

9) This NBA basketball team sets a record for regular season victories, finishing 73-9 and advances to the NBA finals, but loses to Lebron James and the Cleveland Cavaliers 4 games to 3, despite having a 3 games to 1 advantage in the series.

10) The death of this gorilla, the result of Cincinnati Zoo trainers having to restrain the gorilla after a small child falls into the enclosure, leads to a viral Internet phenomenon, making the gorilla one of the most memed animals of all time.

11) In Orlando, American Omar Mateen makes a 911 call where he swears loyalty to ISIS, then proceeds to this gay nightclub, where he goes on a shooting spree, killing 49 and wounding 53 more in the deadliest mass shooting in American history to that point and the worst terrorist attack since 9/11.

12) After test footage of this film leaked online in 2014 and garnered massive positive reviews (and after directors James Cameron and David Fincher endorsed the project), Fox finally releases this superhero comedy. The film will become the highest grossing Rated R film of all time.

13) In a shocking result, the United Kingdom European membership referendum, better known as this, ends with nearly 52% of British voters choosing to leave the EU.

14) The Gotthard Base Tunnel is completed through these mountains, becoming the largest train tunnel in the world at nearly 36 miles (57 kilometers).

15) The lack of diversity in the nominees for the Academy Awards leads this three-word phrase, coined by activist April Reign, to trend. In addition, artists Spike Lee and Jada Pinkett-Smith announce they are boycotting the ceremony, and many push for scheduled host Chris Rock to join the boycott. He does not.

16) A United Nations tribunal concludes that China's claims to historic rights in the South China Sea, based on a map with this three-word feature (now synonymous with Chinese attempts to exercise sovereignty over the South China Sea), are invalid. The tribunal states China has never exercised exclusive control over the area, and the exclusive economic zone provided by the United Nations Convention on the Law of the Sea will continue to apply.

17) A coup attempt against President Erdogan in Turkey led by members of the armed forces, who had formed the Council for Peace at Home, fails. One of the main reasons cited for the coup are Erdogan's government's departure from laicism, also known

as this, a concept enshrined in a 1928 amendment to Turkey's constitution and a critical part of Kemalism.

18) This dark fantasy/horror television show, featuring a pair of brothers hunting monsters, begins its 12th season on the CW, the first CW show to reach a 12th season and the last show on the CW to pre-date the UPN/WB merger. It will run for 15 seasons before it will carry on no more.

19) Dilma Rousseff, president of this South American nation, is impeached and removed from office on charges of corruption and misconduct.

20) During the 2016 American presidential election, a video tape is leaked that shows candidate Donald Trump bragging about being unable to restrain himself from committing sexual assault in the presence of a beautiful woman to this host of *Access Hollywood*. Despite the scandal, Trump will be elected to the presidency.

21) After being accused of sexual harassment by multiple female employees, this CEO of Fox News and 20th Century Fox is forced to resign.

22) Prolonged cash shortages occur in India as a result of the demonetization of this currency in 500 and 1,000 denominations.

23) Missing since 1989, *Beach at Scheveningen in Stormy Weather* and *Congregation Leaving the Reformed Church in Nuenen* by this artist are recovered and returned to their museum in Amsterdam.

24) Having previously won a Pulitzer Prize, this musician receives the Nobel Prize in Literature for "having created new poetic expressions with the great American song tradition."

25) The death of this Supreme Court Justice in February leads to Senate Majority Leader Mitch McConnell blocking President Obama's nomination, hoping that the Republicans will win in 2016 and be able to appoint their own justice.

26) Videos taken and altered by the anti-abortion group Center for Medical Progress are used as evidence in an indictment attempt against this organization in Texas. The grand jury declines to charge the organization, but does recommend charges against David Daleiden, the founder of CMP.

27) At the Summer Olympics in Rio de Janeiro, this sprinter becomes the first man to win the 100m in three consecutive Olympics. He will also win the 200m for a third straight Olympics and will retire with eight Olympic medals, all gold.

28) This Matt Damon-led epic is supposed to create a synergistic tentpole blockbuster, fusing both American and Chinese cinema, although somehow managing to disappoint both American and Chinese audiences. The fantasy piece is dogged by accusations of "whitewashing" and utilizing a "white savior" in a film set in China with a primarily Chinese cast. Both critics and the film's director are quick to point out that Damon is playing a Westerner appropriately, not taking the place of a Chinese cast member, and serves as but a roguish foil to the much more honorable and heroic Chinese characters in the story.

29) Right-wing militants seize the Malheur National Wildlife Refuge in Oregon in retaliation for the incarceration of two men convicted of committing arson on federal land (Two men who disavowed the militants' actions). One man is killed over the standoff, and this leader, a rancher whose father is continuing to battle the federal government over grazing rights, is arrested.

30) At the 2016 Miss Universe pageant, this television host and comedian is forced to apologize on air when he admits he made a mistake by announcing Ariadna Gutierrez as the champion instead of the correct winner Pia Wurtzbach.

𝕽𝖆𝖓𝖉𝖔𝖒 𝕱𝖆𝖈𝖙, 𝕱𝖚𝖓 𝖔𝖗 𝕺𝖙𝖍𝖊𝖗𝖜𝖎𝖘𝖊

The incident at the Malheur National Wildlife Refuge was not the first run-in between Clan Bundy and the federal government. Ammon's father Cliven spent twenty-one years illegally grazing cattle on government land without paying grazing fees. This was despite multiple court orders, and multiple lawsuits being decided against him.

Bundy has stated he does not believe the federal government has any right to own land and has refused to pay grazing fees despite federal land grazing fees being approximately 93% less than that charged by the private market.

The issue came to a head in 2014, when Bureau of Land Management officials attempted to seize the cattle illegally grazing. Bundy put out a call to militia and right-wing paramilitary groups to protect his cattle as part of a "range war." (Bundy's words.) Protestors blocked I-15 for multiple hours, assaulted officers, kicked a police dog, and held weapons aimed at government officials.

The BLM eventually agreed to cease the cattle round-up to diffuse the situation. Bundy became a folk hero temporarily on the mainstream right wing of American politics, until making several comments about race, suggesting that African-Americans would be better off if they were still enslaved rather than living on the government dole. Right-wing television personalities like Glenn Beck and Sean Hannity moonwalked away from supporting Bundy as fast as their mouths could carry them.

It remains unknown as to whether or not anyone pointed out the irony to Bundy of his chastising people receiving federal government welfare while grazing his cows for free on federal land. Some of his detractors will christen Bundy the Welfare Cowboy (a play on the Welfare Queen trope adored by right-wing politicians).

𝕬𝖓𝖘𝖜𝖊𝖗𝖘 𝖔𝖓 𝖙𝖍𝖊 𝕹𝖊𝖝𝖙 𝕻𝖆𝖌𝖊...

Answers

1) El Chapo
2) Shi'a (Shi'ite)
3) *Lemonade*
4) Zika virus
5) Belgium
6) *Pokémon Go*
7) The Panama Papers
8) Rodrigo Duterte
9) Golden State Warriors
10) Harambe
11) Pulse
12) *Deadpool*
13) Brexit
14) The Alps
15) #OscarsSoWhite
16) Nine-dash line
17) Secularism
18) *Supernatural*
19) Brazil
20) Billy Bush
21) Roger Ailes
22) Rupee
23) Vincent Van Gogh
24) Bob Dylan
25) Antonin Scalia
26) Planned Parenthood
27) Usain Bolt
28) *The Great Wall*
29) Ammon Bundy
30) Steve Harvey

𝕴𝖓 2017…

1) In response to the election of Donald Trump, this protest begins the day after Trump's inauguration, the largest single day protest in American history, which is also supported by marches in other countries.

2) The Economic Community of West African States assembles troops from Senegal, Nigeria, and Ghana, which invade this country to depose Yahya Jammeh, who refused to leave office despite losing the presidential election to Adama Barrow.

3) In this highly lauded and successful Spanish golfer's 74th attempt to win a major championship, he finally succeeds, capturing the green jacket at Augusta after a one-hole playoff against Justin Rose.

4) Kim Jong-nam, half-brother to North Korean dictator Kim Jong Un, is assassinated in Kuala Lumpur International Airport by the use of this nerve agent. The assassins who perpetrated the crime will state they believed their actions to be a part of a prank show.

5) The United States military deploys their new most powerful non-nuclear bomb at an Islamic State base in Nangarhar. The bomb is the GBU-43/B Massive Ordinance Air Blast (MOAB); however, the MOAB abbreviation leads to this common nickname for the ordinance.

6) Reporting by the *New York Times* implicates this Hollywood producer in multiple instances of sexual assault and rape, leading to the MeToo movement.

7) After ISIS launches terrorist attacks on the Iranian Parliament and the tomb of this man, the Iranian Revolutionary Guard counters by launching six ballistic missiles into Syrian territory, targeting ISIS forces.

8) At a performance by this American pop singer in Manchester, lone wolf terrorist Salman Abedi, an Islamic extremist believed to be unaffiliated with any terrorist organization, detonates a shrapnel filled IED, killing 23.

9) During the UEFA Champions League Final between Juventus and this Spanish team, 14-time winners of the European Championship, a thief shoots pepper spray into the crowd,

hoping he will be able to steal personal items in the chaos. Instead, he creates a panic and a stampede, which kills 3 and injures 1672 people.

10) Technically a sequel to a 1995 film starring a recently deceased and well-loved comedian, this action vehicle for The Rock becomes a surprise financial and critical hit, earning nearly a billion dollars worldwide and finishing as the fifth highest grossing film of the year.

11) A diplomatic crisis begins in the Persian Gulf as a Saudi Arabia-led coalition of Muslim countries cuts off diplomatic ties with this country as well as essentially blockading it, by closing its only land border and prohibiting aircraft and ships to pass through coalition airspace or territorial waterways. The Saudi demands include devolving Iranian influence in the country and ending any sponsorship of terrorism. Normalization in relations will resume in 2021 when an agreement is brokered with the assistance of the United States and Kuwait.

12) Hoping to strengthen her hand in Brexit negotiations by obtaining a larger majority, this British Prime Minister calls for a snap election. Her Conservative Party, however, loses 13 seats, dropping the Tories below the threshold needed to rule as a single party government and forcing them to form a coalition with the Democratic Unionist Party of Northern Ireland.

13) On the anniversary of the suicide of Joy Division frontman Ian Curtis, this frontman of Soundgarden and Audioslave commits suicide by hanging in a Detroit hotel.

14) A rally entitled Unite the Right descends upon Charlottesville, Virginia to protest the removal of this man's statue. Protestors waving Nazi flags, Confederate flags, and other white nationalist symbols (along with Tiki torches) chant racist and anti-Semitic slogans while being met by thousands of counter-protestors. One Unite the Right participant, James Fields Jr., drives his car into counter-protestors, killing Heather Heyer and injuring 35 others.

15) The government of Myanmar resumes its attempted genocide against this minority group of Burmese Muslims.

16) A new entry in this video game series manages to draw some protest from the American right for using the tagline, "Make America Nazi-free Again." (The plot for the game focuses on an alternative future where the U.S. lost World War II and America is occupied by Nazi Germany.)

17) Hurricane Harvey makes landfall in the United States as a category 4 storm, causing extensive damage to this American city due to severe flooding. Harris County, which contains the affected city, will have 25-30% of its land area submerged.

18) After the Kurdistan region of Iraq votes for independence, Iraqi forces attack the military of Kurdistan, known as this, in an attempt to reclaim the oil-rich areas around Kirkuk.

19) During this country music singer's set at the Route 91 Harvest music festival in Las Vegan, gunman Stephen Paddock opens fire from his room in the Mandalay Bay, killing 60 and wounding hundreds more.

20) The United States withdraws from this United Nations body, an organization whose stated purpose is promoting world peace through international cooperation with a focus on science, the arts, and culture, due to perceived anti-Israeli bias. Israel will withdraw not long after.

21) This doctrine is first incorporated into the Constitution of the Chinese Communist Party, serving as the leader of China's methodology for applying Chinese Marxism to modern life.

22) The sale of the Gothic Revival Mansion located at 10236 Charring Cross Road in Los Angeles, better known as this, is finalized for $100 million. The sale had been agreed to the year previously, but the previous owner retained life rights to remain at the property.

23) With only 43% turnout, this autonomous region of Spain votes in favor of independence by 92% to 8%. The referendum is declared unconstitutional by the Spanish High Courts.

24) This work by Leonardo da Vinci is sold at Christie's auction house for $450 million to a member of the Saudi royal family, supposedly purchasing it for the Abu Dhabi Department of Culture and Tourism. It will later be revealed that he was purchasing the painting for Mohammed bin Salman, who has

kept the piece in storage while waiting for a new museum to be built.

25) On the 50th Anniversary of the film *Bonnie & Clyde*, Faye Dunaway and Warren Beatty come on stage to deliver the Best Picture Oscar at the Academy Awards. After a moment of confusion, Dunaway announces that *La La Land* is the winner. While the producers of *La La Land* begin making their speeches, they are interrupted and informed that the correct winner is *Moonlight*. The confusion came from an accountant with this firm, which tabulates the Oscar votes, handing over the wrong envelope to the presenters.

26) The Nobel Prize in Literature is awarded to this author of *The Remains of the Day*.

27) The Advanced Aerospace Threat Identification Program, a government program that spent five years and $22 million looking into reports of these, is first made public.

28) In a scoreline that will forever haunt the dream of Atlanta Falcons fans, the Falcons are leading by this score with seven minutes remaining in the third quarter of Super Bowl LI, before Tom Brady leads the New England Patriots on the greatest Super Bowl comeback of all time. The game will become associated with the scoreline, and the scoreline will become a shorthand for Super Bowl LI.

29) This former director of the FBI is appointed as a special counsel to investigate possible collusion between the Russian government and Donald Trump's campaign team.

30) This musical from the songwriting team behind *Dear Evan Hansen* and *La La Land*, scoring large with fans via word of mouth if not with critics, becomes something of a sleeper hit. It will end its theatrical run with box office returns of $435 million, all without ever cracking the top 3 at the American box office.

Random Fact, Fun or Otherwise

The AATIP was initiated by Senate Majority Leader Harry Reid with co-sponsorship from Senators Daniel Inouye and Ted Stevens. Reid's sponsorship of the bill fits conspiracy theories nicely as he represented Nevada, which is home to Area 51, a place tied to numerous conspiracy theories including being the resting place of those aliens who crashed in Roswell, New Mexico in 1947.

Despite the seeming conspiracy theorist bent to AATIP, the program was commissioned to do actual science to try to explain unexplained aerial phenomena, which came from United States military aviators and video from on board their aircraft. The program researched and published thirty-eight studies on a range of theoretical scientific explanations, including: tracking of hypersonic vehicles, use of cloaking devises, use of warp drive, discussion of traversable wormholes, and the manipulation of extra dimensions.

In 2020, the Pentagon acknowledged the existence of a successor program to AATIP known as UAPTF (Unidentified Aerial Phenomenon Task Force). Most scientists have concluded that there are very much real-world reasons behind the phenomena, resulting from everything including glitchy code to good, old human error, and unlikely to be alien technology.

Answers on the Next Page...

𝕬𝖓𝖘𝖜𝖊𝖗𝖘

1) Women's March
2) The Gambia
3) Sergio Garcia
4) VX nerve gas
5) Mother of All Bombs
6) Harvey Weinstein
7) Ayatollah Ruhollah Khomeini
8) Ariana Grande
9) Real Madrid
10) *Jumanji: Welcome to the Jungle*
11) Qatar
12) Teresa May
13) Chris Cornell
14) Robert E. Lee
15) Rohingya
16) *Wolfenstein*
17) Houston
18) Peshmerga
19) Jason Aldean
20) UNESCO (United Nations Educational, Scientific and Cultural Organization)
21) Xi Jinping Thought (Xi'ism)
22) Playboy Mansion
23) Catalonia
24) *Salvator Mundi*
25) PricewaterhouseCoopers
26) Kazuo Ishiguro
27) UFOs
28) 28-3
29) Robert Mueller
30) *The Greatest Showman*

𝕴𝖓 2018...

1) For thirty-eight minutes, residents of this American state experience panic as a misunderstanding over a drill leads to an emergency warning going out that states a ballistic missile is inbound.

2) The United States government shuts down as debate on a continuing resolution to fund the government becomes enmeshed with this immigration policy, begun by President Obama, but ended by President Trump.

3) Due to state-sponsored doping, certain competitors at the Winter Olympics in PyeongChang are not allowed to complete under the auspices of their country, instead competing as OAR, which is short for this.

4) Kay Goldsworthy is appointed as the archbishop of Perth in the ecclesiastical province of Western Australia, the first female archbishop in this denomination of Christianity.

5) Former Russian spy- who served the U.K. as a double agent- Sergei Skripal is poisoned in London by this nerve agent along with his daughter Yulia. The Russian government is suspected to be behind the poisoning. Both survive.

6) With the death of the last surviving male, Sudan, this subspecies of Central African ungulates becomes functionally extinct, with only two females surviving.

7) Cinemas are reopened in Saudia Arabia for the first time since 1983, and this acclaimed film from the Marvel Cinematic Universe is the first to be screened.

8) North Korean President Kim Jong Un becomes the first North Korean leader to pass completely though this "no man's land" and into South Korea.

9) The state of Hawaii becomes inundated with "laze," a portmanteau of these two words, after the lower Puna volcanic eruption.

10) A bus carrying the Humboldt Broncos collides with a semi-truck, killing sixteen and injuring thirteen more in Saskatchewan. As part of the public outpouring of sympathy, people place these

items outside their doors because, "The boys might need them…
wherever they are."

11) The wedding of this couple is estimated to cost £32 million, but
    will add £500 million to 1 billion to the British economy from
    tourism and souvenirs.

12) In a public referendum, the citizens of Ireland vote by a nearly
    2/3's majority to repeal the 8th amendment to the constitution (an
    amendment also approved by referendum and winning with a 2/3
    majority), which outlawed this.

13) An eighteen-year dispute between Greece and this Balkan
    country (and former member of Yugoslavia) is resolved by the
    addition of a directional modifier. This allows the former
    Yugoslavian state to join NATO and the European Union.

14) In only their second Stanley Cup Final in 44 years of existence, the
    Washington Capitals, led by this Russian-born Conn Smythe
    Trophy-winning captain, defeat the expansion team Vegas
    Golden Knights in five games.

15) Ethiopia agrees to cede the town of Badme to this country, and
    the two countries agree to terms to end a twenty-year long border
    conflict.

16) After reporting that a data breach has led to a slowdown in new
    user growth, this company whose stock ticker symbol will be
    changed to META in 2021, experiences a 20% drop in stock price,
    losing $109 billion in value, the largest loss in corporate history.

17) Inside the Saudi consulate in Istanbul, this journalist for the
    Washington Post is murdered by a Saudi assassination squad,
    allegedly with close ties to Crown Prince Mohammad bin Salman.
    Because Turkish intelligence has bugged the consulate, the attack
    is recorded.

18) This Old West action game from RockStar Games, the third in a
    series which began in 2004, is released to critical acclaim. It will
    go on to sell over 50 million copies and become the 8th bestselling
    video game of all time.

19) Investigators for the Camp Fire California wildfire lay blame for
    the blaze which killed 85 and displaced 85,000 people on faulty
    equipment belonging to this power company.

20) As part of the somber celebrations on the centenary of the ending of World War I, French President Emmanual Macron and German Chancellor Angela Merkel lay a wreath in the Glade of the Armistice in this French city.

21) This nation advances to the final of the FIFA World Cup after winning two games in penalty kicks and one game in extra time in the knockout round, but will lose to France, 4-2.

22) Despite being stabbed in the stomach during a campaign rally, this populist candidate will cruise to an easy victory in the Brazilian presidential election.

23) The United Nations Telecommunication Union reports for the first time that more than half of the world's population has access to and uses this.

24) Thousands of volunteers and government workers come together to free a soccer team trapped in the Tham Luang Nang Non caves in this country. The entire team will be rescued, but two rescuers will be killed, one on scene and one a year later from an infection acquired during the rescue.

25) The Russian Coast Guard captures three Ukrainian vessels attempting to navigate this body of water connecting the Black Sea and the Sea of Azov.

26) This novel from Delia Owens, serving as both a coming-of-age story and a mystery novel, leads to an increase in Google searches regarding crayfish.

27) During the Weekend Update segment on *Saturday Night Live*, this comic pokes fun at new Congressman Dan Crenshaw, who wears an eyepatch due to losing an eye in combat while a Navy SEAL. Protests come in immediately from the right and from Crenshaw himself, who will receive an apology on the next week's episode when he does a cameo.

28) This Queen of Soul passes away at the age of 76 in Detroit. When Fox News reports her passing, they will use an image of Patti LaBelle on accident.

29) Economic protests begin in Paris over high fuel prices and increased wealth inequality. The protests and the protestors

become named after the garments they wear, a garment required to be kept in French vehicles per a 2008 law.

30) This Swedish ninth grader begins striking from school in order to call attention to the climate crisis. Initially a novelty, within a year, millions of students across the world will be following suit.

Random Fact, Fun or Otherwise

The dispute between Greece and Macedonia over the name of the latter might seem like a rather small concern in the grand scheme of things, not necessarily the kind of thing that should throw off economic and military alliances like NATO and the EU. However, the Greeks may have had some good points.

Firstly, historic Macedonia, i.e. the Greek Kingdom of Macedon of Alexander the Great, is located almost entirely within modern day Greece. Greeks quite rightly view the achievements of Macedonian culture and Alexander the Great as an important part of Greek history, and the cultural appropriation of that name and symbols like the Vergina Sun are not looked favorably upon. Secondly, allowing the Republic of Macedonia to keep its name might lead to an irredentist attempt the create a greater Macedonia, incorporating areas of Greece, Macedonia, Albania, Serbia, and Bulgaria, similar to the Greater Albania movement.

The Republic of Macedonia's contention was that Macedon was not culturally or politically Greek or was at least only distantly related, and that modern Greek Macedonia only came into being after a period of Hellenization in the early 20th century.

In the end the new name of North Macedonia was overwhelmingly approved in a referendum and in the Macedonia Assembly.

Answers on the Next Page...

𝕬𝖓𝖘𝖜𝖊𝖗𝖘

1) Hawaii
2) DACA (Deferred Action for Childhood Arrivals)
3) Olympic Athletes from Russia
4) Anglicanism (Church of England)
5) Novichok
6) Northern white rhinoceros
7) *Black Panther*
8) Demilitarized Zone
9) Lava & haze
10) Hockey sticks
11) Prince Harry & Megan Markle
12) Abortion
13) North Macedonia
14) Alex Ovechkin
15) Eritrea
16) Facebook
17) Jamal Khashoggi
18) *Red Dead Redemption 2*
19) Pacific Gas & Electric Company
20) Compiegne
21) Croatia
22) Jair Bolsonaro
23) The Internet
24) Thailand
25) Kerch Strait
26) *Where the Crawdads Sing*
27) Pete Davidson
28) Aretha Franklin
29) Yellow vests
30) Greta Thunberg

𝔍𝔫 2019...

1) Bartholomew I, the ecumenical patriarch of this city- a city which exists only by another name- and leader of the Orthodox Church, follows through on his promise to grant self-governorship to the Ukrainian Orthodox Church, making it independent of the Russian Orthodox Church. This is met with protest from Russia.

2) While President Ali Bongo is receiving medical treatment in Morocco, members of the armed forces of this country announce they are staging a coup after seizing control of the national television station in Libreville. The coup attempt is quickly ended.

3) At the FIFA Women's World Cup group stage, this American striker scores five goals in the USA's 13-0 victory against Thailand. She will miss out on the Golden Boot, however, losing to teammate Megan Rapinoe.

4) A political crisis erupts in Venezuela with incumbent President Maduro and challenger Juan Guaido both claiming to be the victors in the 2018 presidential election. After Maduro is sworn in for a second term, this international organization founded in 1948, which incorporates all major countries in North and South America save Cuba, issues a statement declaring Maduro's presidency to be illegitimate.

5) *Chang'e 4*, a space mission launched by this country, becomes the first to achieve a soft landing on the far side of the Moon.

6) After committing to do multiple *Avatar* sequels, director James Cameron taps this director of *El Mariachi* to helm a long simmering project, *Alita: Battle Angel*.

7) Dogfights break out over this disputed territory in Asia between the Indian Air Force and the Pakistani Air Force as India attempts to retaliate for a jihadist terrorist attack launched by militants from the Pakistani side of the border. One Indian fighter is shot down with the pilot safely ejecting.

8) After two crashes in five months due to issues with the new Maneuvering Characteristics Augmentation System, 387 of these aircraft are grounded by the FAA and other national regulating bodies.

9) In an interesting case of nominative determinism, Senior VP of the American branch of this video game company Doug Bowser replaces retiring CEO Reggie Fils-Aimé.

10) Australian white supremacist Brenton Tarrant goes on a shooting spree, killing 51 and wounding 40 in two mosques in this Oceanic city. He is on his way to a third mosque when his vehicle is rammed by the police.

11) Nursultan Nazarbayev resigns from his post of president of this country, which he has held since the breakup of the Soviet Union in 1991. Having ruled as an autocrat, he handpicks a successor who unsurprisingly wins a snap presidential election.

12) This cast member of the television show *Empire* stages a hate crime with the help of two extras from his show, and claims he was attacked by two white males who shout Trumpist mottos, use racial and homophobic slurs, douse him in chemicals, and tie a noose around his neck.

13) The Event Horizon Telescope successfully captures an image of one of these stellar phenomena for the first time, this one sitting in the center of a galaxy named Messier 87.

14) Founder of WikiLeaks Julian Assange has his asylum in this country's London embassy revoked, and he is arrested by British authorities. Both Swedish and American authorities have unveiled charges against him and are attempting to extradite him.

15) The family of this deceased author, who served as inspiration for characters played by James Earl Jones in 1989 and Sean Connery in 2000, announce they are editing all of his unpublished work with intents to publish it soon.

16) Due to multiple mistakes- a guard being sent to the wrong area to investigate a fire alarm and the fire alarms being incapable of notifying authorities- this Parisian landmark burns for 43 minutes before firefighters arrive on the scene.

17) Volodymyr Zelenskyy wins the Ukrainian presidential election, running as a member of this party- a party that takes its name from a Ukrainian television show, which starred Zelenskyy as a common man who surprisingly wins the Ukrainian presidential election.

18) This conservative political consultant is charged with seven counts of witness tampering and obstruction of justice. Although sentenced to 40 months in jail, his sentence is commuted by President Trump, and he will eventually receive a full pardon.

19) Victor Vescovo sets a record for largest lifetime change in elevation without leaving the Earth, having already climbed 29,029 feet to the top of Mount Everest in 2010 and descending to Challenger Point, the lowest point on the Earth's surface, located underwater in this formation.

20) With the abdication of his father Akihito, Naruhito accedes to the throne of Japan, a throne known as this.

21) This film from director Todd Phillips becomes the first Rated R film to break the $1 billion box office mark and inspires discussion regarding mental health and the psychology of murderers and mass killers.

22) Suthida Tidjai, a former flight attendant, becomes Queen of Thailand after becoming the 4th wife of King Vajiralongkorn. Prior to their marriage, Suthida had served Vajiralongkorn in this capacity.

23) The 2019 World Series, won 4 games to 3 by the Washington Nationals, triggers some celebration in this Canadian city, the previous home of the Nationals.

24) The United States House of Representatives begins this kind of inquiry into President Trump as a result of his attempts to strongarm Ukrainian president Volodymyr Zelenskyy into investigating Hunter Biden in exchange for Trump authorizing military aid to Ukraine.

25) Wildfires break out in this archipelago off the coast of Morrocco, owned by Spain.

26) A trade dispute begins between these two Asian democratic nations, allegedly resulting from sanction-violating trade practices. In reality, the argument probably stems from enmity and unresolved issues brewing since 1910.

27) Theresa May resigns as the leader of the U.K. Conservative Party (the Tories), officially ending her reign as Prime Minister,

triggering a battle between Jeremy Hunt and this former Mayor of London for leadership of the party.

28) Google claims their supercomputer has solved problems in 200 seconds that would take an existing supercomputer 10,000 years to solve, thereby achieving a landmark in computing, coined this by John Preskill. IBM will dispute the claim, suggesting a supercomputer could complete the problems in 2.5 days.

29) Back-to-back months with mining or sabotaging of oil tankers in this body of water, transiting from the Persian Gulf to the Indian Ocean, leads to heightened tensions between the United States and Iran, whom the U.S., U.K., and Saudi Arabia blame for the attacks on shipping.

30) Protests begin in Hong Kong as a newly proposed law threatens to allow Hong Kong citizens to be extradited to mainland China, which violates this constitutional principle in the People's Republic of China's governance of Hong Kong and Macau.

Random Fact, Fun or Otherwise

A week before the alleged "attack," Jussie Smollett had received a latter via the *Empire* studio, which contained a crude drawing of a man being lynched, death threats, and a white powder, later determined to be Tylenol. After reports of the attack surfaced, politicians on both sides of the aisle condemned the attack vociferously, although some questioned the story.

Two weeks later, the police raided the home of two Nigerian brothers who worked as extras on *Empire*. They found bleach and other evidence on the scene, but did not charge the brothers after evidence provided during their interrogations. Two days later, the news broke that the brothers had been paid $3500 to help stage the attack.

The brothers stated that Smollett staged the attack when the letter incident did not garner the publicity he hoped for. (Police investigated whether Smollett sent the letter to himself, but it has not been determined conclusively.) They also claimed that Smollett chose the location for the attack- in full view of several security cameras, instructed the brothers on the clothes to wear, to fashion a noose, and to pour gasoline on him (which was later changed to bleach).

Allegedly, Smollett became angry when his agent called the police, whom he did not want involved. The police claim he also became very upset when told that the cameras did not actually capture the attack.

In the end, Smollett was charged with six counts of disorderly conduct, convicted, and sentenced to 150 days in jail and required to pay $120,000 in restitution.

Answers on the Next Page...

𝕬𝖓𝖘𝖜𝖊𝖗𝖘

1) Constantinople
2) Gabon
3) Alex Morgan
4) Organization of American States
5) China
6) Robert Rodriguez
7) Kashmir
8) Boeing 737 MAX
9) Nintendo of America
10) Christchurch
11) Kazakhstan
12) Jussie Smollett
13) Black hole
14) Ecuador
15) J.D. Salinger
16) Notre-Dame
17) Servant of the People
18) Roger Stone
19) Marianas Trench
20) Chrysanthemum Throne
21) *Joker*
22) Bodyguard
23) Montreal
24) Impeachment
25) Canary Islands
26) South Korea & Japan
27) Boris Johnson
28) Quantum Supremacy
29) Gulf of Oman
30) "One country, two systems"

In 2020...

1) The Covid-19 pandemic, which is believed to have originated in this city (either in a wet market or in a government lab), dominates news headlines and impacts almost every aspect of life around the globe.

2) Militants in multiple countries, such as Yemen, the Philippines, and Syria, answer the call of this U.N. Secretary General for a ceasefire. Some will accept offered medical aid in exchange.

3) The NBA season resumes after the Covid interruption with the Finals contested at Walt Disney World, which received this nickname during the contest.

4) Wildfires dramatically affect this state in Australia, home to Sydney and a large percentage of the Australian population, many of whom are affected by the massive decrease in air quality. 445 people die from smoke inhalation.

5) In retaliation for planning and leading attacks on American army bases in Iraq in 2019, the American Air Force uses this model drone to attack a convoy carrying Iranian Major General Qasem Soleimani who leads the Quds Force, the Revolutionary Guard's clandestine and asymmetric warfare force. Soleimani is killed.

6) A copy of this William Shakespeare play, his last, is found in a library in Salamanca, Spain and dated to 1634. It is believed to be the oldest copy of any Shakespeare work.

7) The Libyan Civil War ends in a ceasefire as the Libyan National Army based out of this city serving as their capital, a city which changed hands multiple times in World War II, are unable to conquer the capital of the Government of National Accord, Tripoli.

8) At the impeachment trial of Donald Trump, this Senator from Utah becomes the first and only Senator to ever vote to convict a president from his own political party.

9) This actor dies of colon cancer after battling the disease for four years. He will be nominated for an Academy Award for best actor in his final film role in *Ma Rainey's Black Bottom*, but despite the awards show apparently set up to end the night with his victory, he does not win.

10) The free trade agreement known as USMCA is signed into law, replacing the 1996 free trade agreement known by this acronym.

11) On March 9, the Dow Jones Industrial Average falls 2,000 points, the largest ever intraday fall, triggering these automatic trading pauses designed to curb panic selling.

12) Armed protestors enter this state's statehouse, demanding an end to Covid-19 lockdown restrictions.

13) Setting the stage for the dramatic fall of the U.S.-supported Afghan government, the United States and the Taliban sign a peace agreement in this capital city of Qatar. Per the agreement, the U.S. curtails the number of airstrikes used against the Taliban, removing the Afghan government's best weapon against the Taliban, who will take control of Afghanistan in just one year.

14) These two nations begin an oil price war, which causes prices to plummet. The war does not end until President Trump specifically requests that the countries cut production to help stabilize oil prices.

15) This long-time game show host passes away after a battle with pancreatic cancer. Please state your answer in the form of a question.

16) The Likud Party and the Blue and White Party agree to a power-sharing arrangement in this Israeli governmental body, but the coalition government falls apart in less than a year.

17) After the death of this basketball player in a helicopter accident, multiple teams began their subsequent games with 8-second violations and 24-second violations in tribute, 8 and 24 both being numbers the player wore.

18) The *BepiColombo* mission co-sponsored by the European Space Agency and the Japan Aerospace Exploration Agent sets off on its mission to this planet, where it should arrive in 2025.

19) In order to combat the coronavirus and spur the development of a vaccine, the Trump administration launches a public-private partnership named this.

20) This CEO becomes the first human to have wealth of $200 billion, despite a costly divorce just 1 year previous.

21) The Falkland Islands are declared to be free of these munitions, 38 years after the war ended.

22) In the first crewed orbital flight launched from the United States since the end of the space shuttle program, astronauts Douglas Hurley and Robert Behnken ride a spacecraft named *Endurance*, one these SpaceX ships.

23) President Erdogan of Turkey orders this former cathedral, former mosque, and current museum constructed on the order of Justinian I in 537 to be reverted to a mosque.

24) This American bank agrees to pay a $3 billion fine as a result of a scandal in which employees were pressured to create fake accounts in the names of their customers.

25) The United States designates this ultranationalist, white supremacist, paramilitary group a terrorist organization, the first white supremacist group to receive the designation.

26) Protests break out in Belarus as this incumbent president declares himself the victor in his bid for a sixth term, despite widespread belief in election irregularities and accusations of fraud.

27) After receiving an endorsement from Representative Jim Clyburn, the flagging campaign of Joe Biden receives a boost as he wins this state in the Democratic presidential primary.

28) Agents of this Russian department are revealed to have been paying bounties to the Taliban for murders of American soldiers. Despite being briefed on the issue, President Trump orders no response.

29) After the murder of this man by Minneapolis police officers, protests against racism, police brutality, and police militarization break out across the United States, soon joined by the rest of the world.

30) Entomologists and wildlife control agents rush to stop an incursion of Asian giant hornets, known as these in the media, in the Pacific Northwest.

Random Fact, Fun or Otherwise

The required lockdowns changed a lot about life, and it is interesting to reflect on all the strange things that happened in that time:

- Zoom took over the planet. (How did Skype lose this battle?)
- Hoarding Toilet Paper or Various Cleansers
- Washing groceries.
- The cringy celebrity cover of "Imagine."
- How easily so many corporate cultures adapted to what they always said was impossible: working from home (And how they are now trying to go back).
- *Tiger King*/Carole Baskin
- People baking bread, especially sourdough
- TikTok Dance trends
- RV Vacations & Van Life
- Priest baptizing babies via water pistol
- John Krasinski's *Some Good News*
- Makeshift PPE
- Dalgona Coffee
- Playing *Among Us*
- Good *Community* and *Parks & Rec* reunions, and a pretty lousy *30 Rock* one.

Answers on the Next Page...

Answers

1) Wuhan
2) Antonio Guterres
3) "The Bubble" (The NBA Bubble)
4) New South Wales
5) MQ-9 Reaper (Reaper)
6) *The Two Noble Kinsman*
7) Tobruk
8) Mitt Romney
9) Chadwick Boseman
10) NAFTA
11) Circuit breakers
12) Michigan
13) Doha
14) Russia & Saudi Arabia
15) Who is Alex Trebek?
16) Knesset
17) Kobe Bryant
18) Mercury
19) Operation Warp Speed
20) Jeff Bezos
21) Land mines
22) Crew Dragon
23) Hagia Sophia
24) Wells Fargo
25) Russian Imperial Movement
26) Alexander Lukashenko
27) South Carolina
28) GRU
29) George Floyd
30) Murder hornets

The Ministry of Trivia Thanks You

**All Rights Reserved
to Whomever They Belong.**

**No rain checks, no guarantee of enjoyment,
no Cash on Delivery.**

Proof of Purchase not Available on Request.

**All Warranties Void
Outside of the Terrestrial Realm.**

**To Conclude with *God Bless America*
in Full Chorus.**

**Thank you for completing
this unit of entertainment.
Your participation has been
noted in your permanent file.**

About the Author

Justin Bohardt became a writer because he realized early in life that creating alternative realities was infinitely preferable to living in the existing one. A former reporter, he moonlights as an employee for a Fortune 100 insurance company while crafting new worlds in every second of free time he can find.

He is the author of numerous novels in the fields of science fiction and fantasy, some novellas that flirt with being literary fiction, collections of short stories and poetry, and the occasional rom-com. His fiction has appeared in numerous magazines that no longer exist, but were kind enough to pay in cash.

He resides on planet Earth (for the time being) with his family.

Please visit him online at: http://gggeflat.wix.com/justinbohardt

Also by the Author

The Ministry of Trivia
  A Century of Trivia
The Parliament of the Profane Series:
  Summum Omnium Bonus
  Fides Uberrima
  Gloria Deo
The Invasion of Miraval Series:
  Partisan
  Guerrilla
  Saboteur
Infinite Universe Series:
  111 Souls
  48 Traitors (Coming Soon)
Manic Sonata
A Mercenary of Palladia Series:
  No Songs Are Sung
  Of His Sword
Story Collections:
  Sanguine Starscapes
  Reality & Other Falsehoods
  Tales from an Altered Verse
Kindle Vella Stories:
  Reunion
  The Waking Nightmares of Vincent Green
  The Mysteries of Havenhearth
  All the Voices Speak as I
  The Lantern
  Aetherium
  Archetypes & Orphans

  Available exclusively at Amazon.com!

www.ingramcontent.com/pod-product-compliance
Lightning Source LLC
Chambersburg PA
CBHW050827260726
48660CB00004B/1646